Grammar Galaxy

Adventures in Language Arts

Yellow Star

Melanie Wilson, Ph.D.

Rebecca Mueller, Illustrator

Dedicated to future guardians of Grammar Galaxy and to the glory of God.

Special thanks to my family, friends, and to Rebecca Mueller for their invaluable help and support. You made Grammar Galaxy a reality.

Table of Contents

Table of Contents 3

A Note to Teachers 1

Prologue 2

Unit 1: Adventures in Literature 3

Chapter 1 4

Chapter 2 11

Chapter 3 17

Chapter 4 23

Chapter 5 28

Chapter 6 34

Chapter 7 39

Unit 1I: Adventures in Spelling & Vocabulary 44

Chapter 8 45

Chapter 9 50

Chapter 10 57

Chapter 11 64

Chapter 12 69

Chapter 13 74

Chapter 14 80

Unit III: Adventures in Grammar 85

Chapter 15 86

Chapter 16 91

Chapter 17 95

Chapter 18 103

Chapter 19 107

Chapter 20 113

Chapter 21 119

Chapter 22 126

Chapter 23 133

Chapter 24 139

Chapter 25 145

Chapter 26 150

Unit 1V: Adventures in Composition & Speaking 156

Chapter 27 157

Chapter 28 163

Chapter 29 169

Chapter 30 176

Chapter 31 182

Chapter 32 188

Chapter 33 194

Chapter 34 200

Chapter 35 205

Chapter 36 209

About the Author...212

About the Illustrator..213

A Note to Teachers

I'm passionate about language arts. I love to read, write, and speak. As a homeschooling mom, I wanted my own children and my friends' children to share my passion. Over the years, I found aspects of many different curricula that clicked with my students. But I never found something that did everything I wanted a complete curriculum for elementary students to do:

- Use the most powerful medium to teach language arts: story
- Give the why of language arts to motivate students
- Teach to mastery rather than drill the same concepts year after year
- Limit seat work and use little-to-no-prep games to teach instead
- Teach literary concepts, vocabulary, spelling, writing & speaking

I felt called to create my own fast, easy, and fun curriculum for homeschooling parents and others who want to see students succeed in language arts.

Grammar Galaxy: Yellow Star is for students who are at about a fourth-grade level or have completed *Nebula* and *Protostar* or the equivalent. *Yellow Star* can be read and completed independently if your student is at a 3rd grade reading level. The stories and concepts are appropriate for students in first to sixth grade, however, making this a perfect read-aloud for families. If you are reading to your student, be sure to point out the synonyms for vocabulary words that are provided. Following each story, there are questions to check for understanding. Students should complete the corresponding mission in the *Mission Manual* before moving on to the next story. The *Mission Manual* can be purchased at GrammarGalaxyBooks.com/shop.

My hope is that your student will accept the call to be a guardian of Grammar Galaxy.

Melanie Wilson

Prologue

The king of Grammar Galaxy tried not to worry. He had made his three children, Kirk, Luke, and Ellen English, guardians of the galaxy. Together with the other young guardians on planet English, they had defeated the Gremlin and saved the English language many, many times. Words and punctuation marks were returned to their planetary homes, destructive laws were changed, and the kids had learned a lot about literature, grammar, and writing.

But would the Gremlin's schemes finally get the best of them? Would they eventually face a crisis they couldn't overcome with the help of *The Guide to Grammar Galaxy*? He didn't know. He asked Screen for a status report on the galaxy. All seemed well for the moment.

Unit I: Adventures in Literature

Chapter 1

Luke had just finished story time at the library. The librarians had asked him to continue storytelling because the younger kids loved his stories. Luke enjoyed doing it, even though it took him time.

He decided to pick out some new books before returning home. He browsed through the stacks and opened a book that seemed very interesting. The entire thing was made up of pictures. The characters' words were written in clouds next to them. Luke was **entranced** until he heard one of the mothers who had attended story time talking to her friend.

★ ★ ★ ★ ★ ★ ★ ★ ★ ★

entranced– *captivated*

★ ★ ★ ★ ★ ★ ★ ★ ★ ★

"Ugh. Comic books. I want my Jimmy to read real books. These are like junk food. They're not good for kids." Her friend nodded in agreement.

Luke closed the book he was holding and put it back on the shelf. He wasn't surprised to learn that the book was a junk book. It seemed so cool and fun to read. He should be reading more serious books. He was a guardian of the galaxy after all.

He moved to the nonfiction section and began browsing. He found a book on spaceball Hall of Famers he was eager to read. But he really wanted a new fiction book too. He wandered to the fiction section, determined to find a new book. He paged through a few titles, but they seemed dull in comparison to the comic book. He walked back to the stack he had been in earlier and looked around to make sure the mothers were gone. They were.

He found the book and as he read a bit more of it, he found himself laughing. Maybe it was a junk book, but he liked it. He decided to check it out.

Luke took the two books to the circulation desk to check them out himself. He wouldn't have to explain his selection to the librarian. But she stopped him.

"Let me see what you're checking out, Luke." He handed her the two books reluctantly. "Oh, spaceball. How did your team do last season?"

"Great! We had a winning record," Luke said, smiling. He used the opportunity to reach for the books, but the librarian was already looking at the second title.

"Oh, you're getting a graphic novel!" she exclaimed. Luke was confused but nodded slowly. "Thanks again for leading story time, Luke. We're so grateful to have you," she said, handing him the books.

"Oh. No problem. I like doing it," he said. He eagerly took the books from her, scanned them, and stuffed them into his book bag.

The librarian said goodbye and Luke walked home quickly. When he arrived, he realized he was starving and stopped in the kitchen for a snack.

Cook greeted him warmly. "How did the storytelling go?" she asked.
"Really good."
"I think you're meaning to say well," Cook corrected him.
"Really well," Luke said with a mouth full of cookie.
"Now you're talking with your mouth full again."
"Sorry," Luke said, still chewing.

Cook couldn't help but laugh. Luke drank some milk and realized he could ask Cook about the junk book he'd checked out.

"Cook, what does *graphic* mean?"

"Oh, my word, why are you asking me vocabulary questions?" she said. But it was clear the question pleased her. "*Graphic* means something shown in great detail. For example, a movie with graphic violence is something a young man like you ought not to see."

"Or read? Should I not read graphic books?" Luke asked.

"You should ask your parents, of course, Luke. But you're awfully young to be reading graphic violence. Once you read it, you have a picture in your mind that doesn't soon leave."

Luke nodded thoughtfully. "Thank you – for the cookie and the vocabulary lesson." He smirked and Cook ruffled his hair.

Luke took the books to his room. He decided that he wouldn't read the graphic novel. He knew his parents wouldn't approve. He started reading the spaceball book instead. He enjoyed reading the impressive stats of the Hall of Famers. He daydreamed about becoming a Hall of Famer himself and fell asleep.

He forgot what he had been doing before his nap. When he remembered, he also remembered the graphic novel. The book hadn't seemed that violent. If it was violent, he could handle it. He had to be prepared for violence if an alien war happened, right?

He removed the graphic novel from his bag and opened it to the beginning. It was all about Spaceman. He had been born on a planet that had been **demolished** by one of his sworn enemies. One of the pictures showed the planet exploding in a fireball. *This must be the graphic violence Cook was talking about,* he thought.

★ ★ ★ ★ ★ ★ ★ ★ ★ ★

demolished– *destroyed*

abruptly– *suddenly*

★ ★ ★ ★ ★ ★ ★ ★ ★ ★

He was so immersed in the story that he didn't notice that Kirk had come in. "I came to see if you wanted to play tennis with us," he said.

Luke **abruptly** closed the book and jammed it into his book bag. "Uh, maybe. I might. Yes," he stammered.

"What were you reading?" Kirk asked.

"A book," he answered.

"I can see that. Which book?" Kirk pressed.

"One I got from the library today."

"You're acting weird. Are you going to play tennis with us or not?"

Luke agreed and left with Kirk. *That was a close one*, he thought. *Kirk would definitely tell Father I was reading a graphic novel. I have to be careful to read it where I won't be caught. I'm plenty old enough to read this book.*

That night Luke finished the Spaceman book. He loved it. *Why is everything I like bad for me?* Luke grumbled to himself. He disagreed that he shouldn't read it, but he wanted to return the book to the library as soon as possible. It wouldn't do for his mother to find it.

After turning the book in at the library, he couldn't help but look for another Spaceman book. He was delighted to find there were many of them. He was also pleased that he had come up with a way to read them without being caught. He would stay at the library to read!

He found a comfortable chair to read in and went on another adventure with Spaceman. He was enjoying himself so much that he didn't hear the announcement that the library was closing. The librarian interrupted him to tell him.

He reluctantly went to put the book back on the shelf. But how could he wait to see if the Invader succeeded in killing Spaceman? He couldn't. He decided to check the book out and finish it at home. He would have to find a good place to read it in secret.

At home, Luke knew he should wash his hands and get ready for dinner. But he couldn't stand it. He had to know what happened. He decided to go to the cellar for just a few minutes. He would be done in plenty of time for dinner.

The lighting wasn't good, and it smelled funny in the cellar. Luke didn't care. He read a whole chapter using his reading light. The quiet and darkness somehow made the story even more exciting. He didn't hear the creaking of the stairs or anything until Cook screamed. "My word, boy, you scared me nearly to death. Why are you reading down here?"

Luke stammered, and Cook's eyes narrowed. "Are you reading a graphic book?" Luke's face gave her the answer. "I told you not to."

"I know," Luke whispered guiltily.

Cook clucked her tongue. "You know I have to tell your parents." Luke nodded and hung his head.

The rest of the family was seated at the dining table when Cook and Luke came into the room. "I'm sorry to report that I found Luke reading a graphic book. He had asked me about it and I told him it wasn't right for a boy his age."

"That's what you were reading!" Kirk exclaimed before the king could respond.

"I'm surprised that you ignored Cook's advice," the king said. "Let me have a look at the book," he demanded.

Luke shamefully handed it over and didn't look up until the king laughed heartily. "Spaceman? That's the graphic book you're reading?"

Luke was shocked by his reaction but nodded.

"Spaceman was my favorite when I was your age," the king said fondly.

"But it's graphic, right? The librarian said so."

"It's a graphic novel. That's not the same thing as a book with graphic content." The king called for *The Guidebook to Grammar Galaxy* to be brought to him. He shared the entry on graphic novels with the family.

Graphic Novels

"Graphic novel" is used to describe a book's format and not its genre. There are both fiction and nonfiction graphic novels. Graphic novels are long comic books with images in a sequence. The images, word balloons, and thought balloons are typically contained in boxes called panels. Like other books, graphic novels are read left to right and top to bottom.

Words and sentences in graphic novels are sometimes written in capital letters. Multiple exclamation and question marks are also used to express strong emotion.

This comic explains what a graphic novel is.

The king stopped and had the children look at the graphic novel comic.

©Jessica Abel http://dw-wp.com. Used with permission.

"So, I didn't do anything wrong? What a relief!" Luke exclaimed.

"Oh, I didn't say that," the king answered. We should always know what you're reading, Luke. Some books are too mature for you. Others teach things that don't fit our values. You should have asked us about the book right away."

"You're right. I'm sorry. I heard a mother at the library say it was a junk book that wasn't good for kids. But I liked it. I thought you wouldn't approve," Luke explained.

"That's the other mistake you made. You thought you knew my opinion without asking me. Some teachers have believed that graphic novels aren't real books. At least they believed they weren't as valuable as other novels. We now know that reading is reading. The pictures and short sections of dialogue are motivating for kids. I didn't even like to read before I read Spaceman." Cook and the rest of the family gasped. "It's true," he said.

"Father, I will definitely tell you what I'm reading from now on," Luke said apologetically.

"And listen to me too, I hope," Cook teased.

"Yes," Luke said grinning. "I wonder if I'm the only one who thinks graphic novels are bad."

"I think we have another mission," Kirk said.

The three sent out a mission called "Graphic Novels" after dinner.

What does *entranced* mean?

What is a graphic novel?

What did Luke's father say he did wrong?

Chapter 2

The castle was eerily quiet. The king hadn't heard or seen his three children all day. He found his wife in her study and asked where they were.

"Oh, don't you remember, dear? They're preparing for the Book Battle tomorrow."

"That's right. I had forgotten. They're studying hard then? I was hoping to take them all hiking."

"They want to do well and make you proud. They're competing as a team, you know."

"They're on the same team? That's marvelous! When is the awards ceremony?" he asked.

"It's at 5 o'clock in the Library of Parliament auditorium."

"Good! We should be done by dinner and ready to celebrate a win for the royal English team," the king **crowed**.

★ ★ ★ ★ ★ ★ ★ ★ ★ ★

crowed – *boasted*

★ ★ ★ ★ ★ ★ ★ ★ ★ ★

"Dear, you don't know that they'll win," the queen warned.

"They're my children, aren't they?" the king answered. He winked at her and left to take their dog Comet for a walk. *At least he won't be too busy studying*, he thought.

After dinner, the three children told their father they were too busy studying to play board games. He decided to observe their study session in the castle library. He was impressed by their teamwork. Each of them took turns asking the others questions based on the books on their list. This year there were both fiction and nonfiction titles to read and answer questions on.

Luke said he was disappointed Spaceman books weren't on the list. "I'd know every question about those books!"

His father chuckled. "I believe you would, Luke. Do you feel prepared for the battle tomorrow?" the king asked all three of them.

11

The trio nodded. "I do, but I know the questions will be hard," Ellen said.

"They have to be so there's just one winning team," Kirk added.

"I wish they had had book battles when I was your age," the king said.

"You would have gotten a trophy for sure!" Luke exclaimed.

The king grinned appreciatively. "I'll leave you to your studying. Just make sure you go to bed early. You need sleep to be sharp."

"We will," they answered in unison.

The next morning, Cook had sack lunches ready for them. "It's brain food," she said, tapping her head.

"Thanks, Cook!" they said, hugging her.

The queen hurried them to the space tram. It wouldn't be appropriate to use royal transportation to get there quickly. But it wouldn't be appropriate to get there late either.

The queen checked the three of them in, told them to compete honorably, and returned home. She had a lot to do at home, so she decided to use the space porter. No need to mention it to the king, who would think it was **pretentious**.

★ ★ ★ ★ ★ ★ ★ ★ ★ ★

pretentious – *showy*

★ ★ ★ ★ ★ ★ ★ ★ ★ ★

The kids spotted their friends and greeted them. Then they had to take their seats for opening remarks. The tournament director went over the rules. Afterward, he excused the judges to prepare for competitors in the various rooms. Team rankings would be posted to determine who would move on to the final rounds. Teams could assign a representative to answer questions on specific books.

Luke whispered to his siblings which book he wanted to answer questions about. They agreed while trying to hear what the director was saying. He announced room assignments for the teams and then excused everyone.

The judge in the English kids' room had several cards face down on the table. She asked Luke to choose one for that round of questioning. It was the nonfiction, space book he felt most prepared for. He fist pumped and Kirk frowned at him. "Sorry," Luke whispered.

The judge called each team's representative to a podium at the front of the room. Competitors had a tablet and stylus in front of them on which to record their answers. Answers would be automatically saved and scored digitally. The judge instructed competitors to first enter their name on the tablet. She reminded them that teammates were not allowed to help provide answers. Teams caught doing so would be disqualified. She then began the questioning.

Panic seized Luke. She asked how fast astronaut Edward White had been traveling when orbiting with Gemini 4. *Really fast?* he thought. He knew she wanted an exact speed. *Was that in the book?* he wondered. As the room's large timer ran, he guessed. Luke could tell that his brother and sister didn't know the answer either. That was little **solace**. Luke told himself he would know all the rest of the questions.

★ ★ ★ ★ ★ ★ ★ ★ ★ ★

solace – *comfort*

★ ★ ★ ★ ★ ★ ★ ★ ★ ★

When the second question was read, Luke was trembling. He had no idea what the answer was. He would have to guess again. After he had to guess at all the remaining questions for the book, he hung his head and returned to his seat. He'd let Kirk and Ellen down. He only hoped his siblings could save the team.

Ellen patted her brother on the back and whispered that she hadn't known the answers either. Kirk agreed.

Ellen tried to cheer her brothers up when *Number the Stars* by Lois Lowry was selected. "That's mine," she said. "I've got this!"

Her first question was, "On which day of the week did Ellen first stay with Annemarie's family?" She was soon just as alarmed as Luke had been. She didn't know. And the rest of the questions were no easier. She shrugged nervously and made her best guesses.

This sequence was repeated when Kirk took his turn answering questions. When Kirk slumped into his seat in defeat, Luke was suddenly elated. "I know what this is!" He was shushed by the judge, even though the round was over. He whispered, "This is the Gremlin's doing. We studied so hard. We know these books and now for some reason, we don't. That has to be it."

Kirk smiled, relieved. He reached for his communicator to have Screen search for problems in the galaxy. But he didn't have it. He had forgotten that everyone had to turn in communicators when checking in. "Unfortunately, we won't be able to fix the problem until after the battle," he said.

The three went into the hallway, eager to see the names of advancing teams on the screen. They wondered how they could determine winners if no one got the right answers.

When the results appeared, the advancing teams cheered and high-fived one another. The English family team would not be competing in the next round. Kirk frowned. He couldn't believe that winning teams had been selected when no one knew the answers to the questions. He saw one of his friends celebrating and decided to ask him about it.

"You must have had a good round," he told him.

"Yeah," he said humbly. "Sorry you didn't make it, Kirk."

"It's okay. The questions were impossible to answer. Didn't you think so?"

"No. They were what I expected," he answered.

"Well," Kirk said, "good luck in the next round. We'll come watch you."

Kirk, Luke, and Ellen watched the next round and stared at one another as each question was read. They communicated silently that they couldn't answer the questions. Yet the competitors seemed relaxed. They obviously knew at least some of the answers.

The teams advancing to the final round were posted and the three kids watched Kirk's friend's team compete. The questions presented to them seemed equally impossible to answer, at least for the royal English team.

They dreaded their parents' arrival for the awards ceremony. Just as they feared, their father assumed they were in the final round. He covered his disappointment well and applauded the winners as they were announced. Kirk's friend's team took second place. The royal family congratulated them and then made their way to board the space tram. The group was quiet until they arrived home.

"What went wrong?' the king asked, more sharply than he intended. The queen warned him of his tone by patting his shoulder.

"I don't know!" Kirk exclaimed in frustration. "We were prepared. We honestly thought the Gremlin was involved. But his tricks would have affected everyone. I can't believe other people knew the answers to "What instrument could Bando play?""

Luke and Ellen agreed and repeated the questions they thought were particularly difficult.

"Those were the questions?" the king asked. He was shocked. The three nodded. The king called for *The Guidebook to Grammar Galaxy* to be brought to him. When it arrived, he read the entry called "Drawing Conclusions."

Drawing Conclusions

Drawing conclusions (making decisions) about the meaning of what you read is an important part of reading comprehension.

One of the important decisions or conclusions to make about a text is its main idea. Choose the most important point the author is trying to make. The best clues to the main idea of a paragraph are usually in its first and last sentence. Look for the key or main words of these sentences and ignore the details.

A second important decision to make about nonfiction texts is whether it is fact or opinion. Facts can be proven or disproven with evidence. Opinions are feelings and beliefs that don't rely on evidence.

A third important decision to make about a text is cause and effect. A cause is the reason for an event or reaction. The effect is the event or reaction that follows the cause.

Inference is a fourth important decision to make about a text. An inference is a guess or assumption based on the information that is given.

From the following paragraph, we can draw conclusions.

I have always wanted to be an astronaut. It's the most exciting job in the world. I have wanted to be an astronaut ever since I saw a spacecraft lift off in person. If I could choose my suit color, I would choose silver. I am not afraid of something going wrong with the spacecraft. The danger doesn't keep me from wanting to be an astronaut. I can't wait to start my astronaut career when I'm old enough!

The main idea of the paragraph is that the author wants to be an astronaut. A detail is the author's desire to wear a silver suit. The text is opinion and not fact. The statement that being an astronaut is the most exciting job in the world cannot be proven with evidence. The cause of the author's desire to be an astronaut is seeing a liftoff in person. We cannot infer if the author is male or female. But we can infer or assume that the author is not an adult as he or she isn't yet old enough to be an astronaut.

"I remember reading comprehension," Kirk said. "It's understanding what you read."

"That's right, Kirk. And it's an important skill for every guardian," the king replied. "I'm concerned that the Book Battle is more about details than main ideas. You aren't being asked to draw conclusions about what you read but to memorize trivial details. Details aren't important in literature. They're important to criminal investigations, of course," the king explained.

"And party planning," added the queen.

The king hesitantly agreed, then continued. "If you understand the main idea, fact versus opinion, cause and effect, and how to make inferences, you are literature champions. That's true even if you don't win the Book Battle."

"Do you think the other competitors know these things?' Kirk asked.

"We better make sure," the king said.

"We have a mission to write," Kirk answered.

"Okay, but can we eat first? I'm battle weary," Luke said.

Everyone laughed and agreed to have dinner before writing a mission called "Drawing Conclusions."

What does *crowed* mean?

Where should you look in a paragraph for the main idea?

What is an inference?

Chapter 3

"Your paper, Your Majesty," the butler said, handing the newspaper to the sleepy king.

"Thank you," he answered, yawning loudly. He was about to request coffee when he saw it had already been poured for him. He slurped it loudly and unrolled the paper to read a shocking headline: Gremlin Gone.

The king read eagerly.

GREMLIN GONE

We at *The Grammar Gazette* are in receipt of a letter, **ostensibly** from the Gremlin, the arch-enemy of this galaxy. This is the letter in its entirety.

To whom it may concern (which would be everyone in the galaxy):

I have decided to leave Grammar Galaxy. Frankly, you people bore me. I know you'll be excited to hear the news – perhaps no one more than the king. Good riddance, Your Majesty, or is it more proper to say goodbye? I won't have to worry about those useless **formalities** anymore. I'm not sure which galaxy will have the honor of hosting me yet. Somehow, I don't think you'll be needing my forwarding address. One more thing. I'll be taking a few of my pals with me. You can finally have the happy galaxy you've always wanted.

Cheers!
The Gremlin

We have forwarded this letter to the GBI to determine its **veracity**. But for now, it appears that our arch enemy – the one who has been bent on evil, chaos, and destruction – is gone!

The king put the paper down in disgust. "The Gremlin, gone? Never!" He was pacing anxiously when the queen joined him in the sunroom. "Look at this," he said, handing the paper to her.

She read the article quickly. "This is amazing news!" she said, beaming.

"He isn't gone, dear," he said, sneering a little.

"Why can't you just accept this good news?" she asked. "I think we should have a party to celebrate! I can't remember a party the Gremlin hasn't ruined. Remember your birthday party?"

"How could I forget?" the king said, groaning.

"Exactly! The Gremlin has been a menace. And now he's gone. Stop worrying!" she said, hugging her husband. "Let's celebrate." She pecked him on the cheek and waited expectantly.

★ ★ ★ ★ ★ ★ ★ ★ ★ ★
ostensibly – *supposedly*
formalities – *customs*
veracity – *truth*
★ ★ ★ ★ ★ ★ ★ ★ ★ ★

The king sighed and gazed into her eyes. "I tell you what. Let's give it a week. If the Gremlin lets a whole week go by with no crises, we can have a party."

The queen clapped gleefully and went to find Cook to plan.

"Remember, he really has to be gone!" he called after her.

"I know!" she called back, laughing. "He will be."

When word of the Gremlin's departure reached planets Spelling, Vocabulary, and Sentence, spontaneous celebrations broke out. Words danced and sang and demonstrated their joy. The queen showed footage of the celebrating to the king and said, "See? He's really gone."

The king grumbled. He hated getting his hopes up. He retreated to his study and asked Screen for a status report. "Is anything going wrong in the galaxy? Anything?"

"No, Your Majesty. All's well," was the answer each time.

After several days of peace, the king started to wonder. "Could he really be gone?" He resisted the idea. "He'd never leave. He hates the English language too much," he repeated as if to reassure himself.

After five days without crises, the queen cautiously asked permission to go ahead with party plans. She needed time to plan the biggest celebration in Grammar Galaxy history. The king grudgingly agreed. But he hated the thought of his wife being disappointed too.

On the sixth day, though, he was starting to relax. *Could it be true?* he wondered. Maybe he was worrying for nothing and should be celebrating. He decided to find the kids and see what they were up to. He found Luke lying on the sofa in the media room.

"What are you doing, Luke?" he asked.

"Nothing," Luke said, sighing heavily.

"Hm. That's not like you. Do you feel okay?"

"Yeah. I mean yes."

The king didn't seem convinced. He noticed a book on the sofa next to him. "Oh, another Spaceman book. How is it?"

"Okay. It doesn't seem to have as much action as the others I've read. He saved a planet from being destroyed by a meteor though," Luke explained.

"That sounds like a lot of action to me," the king said. Luke didn't appear to agree. "I tell you what. It's been ages since we've played *King of the Galaxy*. Want to play?"

Luke was suddenly enthusiastic. "I'll find the lasers," he said. He asked Screen to start the game.

"I can't wait to take on Sedition and Defiler!" the king exclaimed.

When the game started, Luke and the king destroyed some space junk that came their way. After minutes of the same passed, their enthusiasm waned. "Where are they?" the king asked.

"The game must be broken," Luke said. "It's old."

"Screen, please determine if the game is functioning," the king commanded.

"I have not detected any errors in the game's programming, Your Majesty," Screen reported.

"Well, something is definitely wrong," the king said, exasperated.

"Do you want to watch a movie?" Luke asked. The king reluctantly said yes, not wanting to disappoint his son. "How about *Meteor Man*?" Luke asked pleadingly.

The king smiled, realizing what it meant to him. "Sounds great!"

Luke asked Screen to play the movie. He looked over at his father when it started to see if he was happy about watching. He was.

In the opening scene, Meteor Man walked down the street, commenting to his sidekick on what a peaceful day it was.

"We know that won't last, right, Father? One of his enemies is going to try to destroy the world!" Luke exclaimed.

His father laughed and nodded. The two continued to watch the movie but soon grew bored. "Where's Atlas? Or a new bad guy? This isn't a good Meteor Man movie, is it?" Luke asked.

"No," the king responded, pondering. "It's almost as if there isn't a bad guy in the movie."

Luke looked at his father, eyes wide. "There wasn't a bad guy in King of the Galaxy ... or my Spaceman book! Do you think the bad guys are all gone?"

The king seemed to be thinking the same thing. "The Gremlin said he was taking his pals with him. What if all the villains in the galaxy are gone?"

"That would be great! Wouldn't it?" Luke asked as he saw his father's expression.

"No. It wouldn't. Characters, even those with evil intent, are what make literature, movies, and even video games work. You've seen today how boring they are without bad guys," the king explained.

Luke had to agree. "Now what do we do? Do we try to get the bad guys back?" Luke asked, not expecting yes for an answer.

"Unfortunately, we have to," the king said. "But first we need your brother and sister."

When the two found Kirk and Ellen, they explained their suspicions. The king took them to the library to teach them about characters in *The Guidebook to Grammar Galaxy*.

Character Traits
Character traits in literature are features of personality that are relatively stable. They may be nouns like *clown, daredevil,* or *wise guy.* They can be adjectives like *brave, shy,* or *arrogant.* Some character traits are given in the text. Others may be revealed through a character's actions, emotions, or dialogue.
Character traits are usually discussed in terms of role. A **protagonist** is the main character, also known as the hero. The protagonist wants something, and the **antagonist** stands in the way. The prefix *pro-* means forward. The protagonist moves the story forward. The prefix *ant-* means against. The antagonist works against the protagonist. The protagonist isn't always a good person and the antagonist isn't always a bad guy. Character traits such as honest/dishonest help determine the nature of the protagonist and antagonist.

"Protagonists and antagonists can both have bad character traits, right?" Ellen asked.

"Yes. What are you thinking?" the king asked.

"Could the Gremlin have taken both any bad character with him?"

"Yes, he could have," the king answered.

"Where in the galaxy could they be?" Kirk asked.

"We've had no reports of disturbances across the galaxy. So, they have to be somewhere we don't ordinarily look," the king said, thinking aloud. After a few moments, he exclaimed, "I've got it! Screen, get me footage from the moon. If I'm right, that's where they are."

"Certainly, Your Majesty," Screen replied. Soon a video feed from the moon was displayed for them. There were hundreds of people and creatures gathered for what looked like a wild party. The children exclaimed as they recognized some of the most famous villains in the crowd.

"You're not serious that we have to get them back?" Luke asked.

"I'm afraid I am," the king said gravely. "As strange as it sounds, our galaxy can't survive without villains. I'm going to have Grammar Patrol pick them up from the moon and return them to planet Composition. Then I'm going to need your help."

"We have to fight all those bad guys?" Luke asked, shuddering.

"No," the king said chuckling. "I need your help in creating a file on them. Having a record of their role and character traits will help to protect the galaxy."

"Some of them are really, really bad," Ellen said, trembling.

"I know. But I trust you and the guardians to keep us safe," the king said.

"We have a mission to write on character traits," Kirk declared.

"And I have a mission to deliver the bad news to your mother that there will be no party," the king said.

What does *veracity* mean?

Why was the *King of the Galaxy* game dull?

What is an antagonist?

Chapter 4

"I've been waiting for this!" the king exclaimed as he opened *The Grammar Gazette.* "This park is going to be so popular. People will love me for it, even though that's not why I created it," he said to himself smugly.

The front page of the paper read, "New Space Park Opens to the Public." The king took a moment to appreciate the picture beneath the headline. Snow-capped mountains surrounded a blue-green lake. "Beautiful," the king murmured before reading the article.

NEW SPACE PARK OPENS TO THE PUBLIC

A new space park opens today, and I couldn't be more excited. I love to hike and fish and take pictures. The park will be the perfect place for me to do all three things. The natural beauty of Point of View Park has always been there, but now it's officially a protected area. I can rest easy knowing that this place will always be a perfect retreat for me. The new signage along the park's trails makes it easy for me to choose a hike that fits my schedule. The new observation deck is the perfect place for me to photograph the wildlife native to the area. The shuttle fare to the park is inexpensive, making travel easy on my budget. All in all, the new space park is great news for me!

The king stroked his beard, trying to figure out what was bothering him about the article. The writer clearly liked the park. That was wonderful. The facts were correct. Then it dawned on him. The writer hadn't given him credit at all! Didn't he know that the park was *his* project? That was bad journalism. He was going to have to say something to the editor of the paper. The more he thought about it, the more irritated he became.

When the rest of the family was seated at the dining table for breakfast, he told the queen about the article. "They published an article about Point of View Park."

"And?" she asked expectantly.

"The author liked it."

"That's wonderful! I'm not surprised," she said, all smiles. She stopped when she noticed he seemed unhappy. "What's the problem?"

"He didn't say anything about me," he said, clearly disgusted.

"Oh, dear. Nothing? Surely he knows this was your project? Did he give someone else credit?"

"No, come to think of it."

"Well, I'm sure it was an oversight. We know this was your idea, don't we, children?' the three English kids nodded, hoping to reassure their father.

"When can we go? I can't wait to hike it!" Luke exclaimed. Kirk and Ellen shared Luke's enthusiasm and the king smiled.

"You're right. The park's opening is wonderful news. It doesn't matter that I get the credit. Let's go this weekend!" The royal family chattered excitedly about the trip over breakfast.

Later at dinner, the king asked his family what they had been reading. It had been too long since he had checked in on their book choices.

"I'm reading another Spaceman book," Luke said, frowning.

"What's wrong, Luke? You love Spaceman," the queen said.

"Yes, normally I do. But this one is weird."

"What do you mean 'weird'?" his mother probed.

"It's hard to explain. It's like he isn't the usual Spaceman. He doesn't say, 'I won't let you destroy the planet, Galacto.' It's like he's talking to me, giving me orders."

Kirk laughed. "That sounds funny."

"It's funny weird, not funny ha-ha," Luke replied.

"Maybe you're supposed to feel like a part of the story," Ellen said.

"It is unusual for a graphic novel," the king agreed. "Maybe the author is trying something different with this title. What are you reading, Ellen?"

"I'm reading a book on jewelry making. I thought it would tell me how to make jewelry, but it's more like a description of someone else making it. You know, first she did this, then she did that."

"My book is a little odd too," Kirk admitted. "I'm reading *Diary of a Wimpy Kid*. I thought the diary would be written by the wimpy kid but it's written *about* him. Kind of like your book, Ellen. First he did this, then he did that."

The king thought for a moment. "My newspaper was odd this morning too." He sighed loudly. "I think I know what the problem is and it's a big one." He called for the guidebook and read the entry on point of view to them.

Point of View

Point of view refers to who is telling the story. There are three points of view in literature: first person, second person, and third person.

First-person point of view gives just one character's take on events, usually the protagonist's (main character's). First person uses the pronouns *I*, *me*, and *mine*. First-person point of view is used in diaries and autobiographies but is also used in some novels.

Second-person point of view is the least common. It discusses the reader and uses the pronouns *you* and *your*. Second person is often used in how-to books. Instructions are often written in second person with the *you* pronoun being understood and not written (i.e., *Preheat the oven* instead of *You preheat the oven*).

Third-person point of view describes the action from all the characters' standpoint. But usually, it gives only one main character's thoughts. Third person uses the pronouns *he*, *she*, and *it*. Third person is a common point of view for fiction.

"Point of view? That's the park you just opened, right?" Ellen asked.

"Right. Something is wrong there. We can't wait until the weekend to go. Dear, can you pack quickly for a stay at the park? We can stay in one of the cabins and investigate in the morning," the king said.

The queen agreed and was actually looking forward to the trip, though she was rushed. Soon the family was using the space porter to travel to planet Composition. The family checked into a cabin that the king reserved at the last minute and got into bed as soon as they could.

The next morning, the king consulted a park ranger. "Something is wrong at Point of View. Have you noticed any unusual activity?"

"No, Your Majesty, I haven't," he answered apologetically.

"Father, what was Point of View used for before you opened the park?" Kirk asked.

"Compositions were orchestrated into points of view. They still are. The first-, second-, and third-person pronouns reside here," the king explained.

"I was just thinking. What if the Gremlin got them mixed up? Can we check?" Kirk asked.

"Certainly. It's a bit of a hike to get to their auditorium, so all the better," the king replied.

When the royal family arrived at the auditorium, they immediately saw the problem. The pronouns *I*, *me*, and *you* were sitting in the third-person chairs. The third-person pronouns were sitting in the first- and second-person chairs.

The king asked to see the Point of View maestro, who arrived in the auditorium in his bathrobe. The queen was mortified.

"What's going on?" the king asked in a reprimanding way.

"What do you mean? I'm enjoying a much-needed vacation!" the maestro said **sourly**.

★ ★ ★ ★ ★ ★ ★ ★ ★ ★

sourly – *unpleasantly*

dismissively – *uninterestedly*

★ ★ ★ ★ ★ ★ ★ ★ ★ ★

His retort infuriated the king. The queen began soothing him to prevent a blow-up. He yelled anyway. "Look at what has happened in your absence!"

"Oh, you mean the pronouns taking turns being first person? I received a letter that helped me see the injustice of *I* and *me* always getting to be first," the maestro explained.

"Who wrote the letter?" Kirk interjected, hoping to give his father time to cool off.

"It was from ERPA, I believe," he answered.

"What's ERPA?" Ellen asked.

"I have no idea," the king said **dismissively**.

"It's the Equal Rights for Pronouns Association," the maestro said.

The king was incredulous. "There is no such thing!" he shouted. The pronouns appeared to be upset by the argument.

26

"There is, and I believe in pronouns' rights," the maestro said, straightening his shoulders defiantly. "Now, if you don't mind, I'm going back to my room."

"Mind? I'll say I mind," the king said a little more quietly this time, trying to control his temper. "Maestro, this pronoun rights experiment you've undertaken is ruining books—and the galaxy too! I have no doubt that the letter you received is from the Gremlin himself."

The maestro was ready to object but the king warned him not to with a glare. "You've created a mess that the guardians are going to have to sort out. Even so, I can see that you need a vacation," the king said.

The maestro nodded, relieved that the king was coming around to his way of thinking. "Effective immediately, you are fired," the king announced. The queen would have gasped if she had been surprised, but she knew this was coming. The maestro had been disrespectful.

The maestro marched off to collect his things and the king finally started to calm down. "Children," he began. The children immediately responded with their attention. They didn't want to make their father any angrier than he already was. "You need to send out a mission on point of view to the guardians right away." The three English children nodded. "I'll need to get to work on finding a new maestro."

"Will there be any time to enjoy the park?" the queen asked hopefully.

★ ★ ★ ★ ★ ★ ★ ★ ★ ★

ruefully – *apologetically*

★ ★ ★ ★ ★ ★ ★ ★ ★ ★

The king smiled **ruefully**. "Yes, my dear. We'll get this mess sorted out and then we can relax."

What does *ruefully* mean?

Which point of view uses the pronoun *he*?

Why were the points of view mixed up in books?

Chapter 5

The queen told her husband how quickly time had passed since their last poetry reading festival.

"Indeed!" the king agreed. "Are the children ready to read this time?"

"Absolutely! They have practiced so much I don't think I can stand to hear their poems one more time," the queen laughed.

"Better to practice too much than too little," the king said, smiling. "Which poems are they reading?"

"Kirk has chosen 'The Raven' by Edgar Allen Poe. Would you like me to recite it? I probably could," the queen giggled. "Ellen has chosen

'My Shadow' by Robert Louis Stephenson and Luke chose 'The Pig' by Roald Dahl. I hope 'The Pig' doesn't scare any of the younger children," she continued, frowning.

"Oh, I'm sure it will be fine. Children know that pigs don't eat people," the king reassured her. "It's a funny poem. I love their selections. It will be a splendid night of poetry reading, I'm sure."

"Yes, I always enjoy it," the queen said.

The three English children were nervous about reading their poems but excited too. On their way to the amphitheater in the spacecopter, Luke said he was most excited about getting ice cream afterward. The king agreed that ice cream was a great part of their tradition.

★ ★ ★ ★ ★ ★ ★ ★ ★ ★

incident – *event*

★ ★ ★ ★ ★ ★ ★ ★ ★ ★

The English kids' readings were completed without **incident**, much to the king and queen's relief. In fact, everyone did a wonderful job reading poems. The children discussed their favorite poems of the evening. In the spacecopter ride to the ice cream shop, the queen whispered to her husband that she had been worried the Gremlin would cause problems.

"I was also concerned, dear, but it appears he has left us alone for the evening. Let's just enjoy the peace and the ice cream." He put his arm around his wife and pulled her close. She smiled up at him.

After an enjoyable treat, the royal family returned to the castle and prepared for bed.

Kirk fell asleep instantly. He was exhausted after all the excitement of reading in public. He hadn't been asleep long, however, when he heard a tapping at his chamber door. *That's odd*, he thought. *Perhaps Luke wants something.* He laid quietly, hoping that Luke would give up and go away. He heard no more from the door, so he buried his head in his pillow, determined to get back to sleep.

Shortly thereafter, he heard a tapping again. This time it was at his window. *Must be the wind*, he thought. He climbed out of bed and opened the window to be sure. He reeled at the sight of great black wings flapping in front of him.

Kirk was shocked when he realized that a raven had just entered his room. He rubbed his eyes. "I'm dreaming!" he exclaimed. When the raven didn't disappear, Kirk trembled. "Your name is?" He whispered the question, hoping he would not be answered.

"Nevermore!" the raven said.

"Uh, can you wait here, please?" Kirk said. He was in a panic to get his father's help. He was either losing his mind or something was very, very wrong in the galaxy.

He managed to wake his parents without too much pounding on the door. His father didn't look happy to be up. "What is it, Kirk? I hope it's an emergency," he warned.

"It is. It is! I know this is going to sound crazy, but there is a talking raven in my room," Kirk said wildly.

"There's a talking raven in your room." The king laughed heartily after he repeated it. "My boy, you've been dreaming! And it's no wonder with as many times as you've read Poe's poem."

"No! I thought that too. I promise you I'm not dreaming," he insisted.

The king could see he was very upset, so he agreed to accompany him to his room. He urged the queen to go back to sleep. "No sense both of us being sleep deprived," he said.

When the two of them entered Kirk's room, they found the window shut and no bird. "Where did he go? He was just here!" Kirk shouted.

"Kirk, quiet. You'll wake the whole castle," the king hushed him.

"I promise you there was a talking raven in here," Kirk insisted, a little more quietly.

"I'm sure you saw one, Kirk. I have **vivid** dreams too. Don't worry about it," the king said.

"It just can't be. I made sure I was awake!" Kirk said, starting to doubt himself.

★ ★ ★ ★ ★ ★ ★ ★ ★ ★

vivid – *intense*

erratic– *inconsistent*

★ ★ ★ ★ ★ ★ ★ ★ ★ ★

"Listen, go back to sleep. If he comes back, let me know, okay?"

Kirk's shoulders sagged. "Okay," he agreed.

After the king left the room, Kirk managed to fall asleep after many anxious minutes. His sleep was **erratic** as he continued to see a raven in his dreams.

The next morning as they sat down to breakfast, the king and Kirk laughed about his vision of a talking raven. "I guess I overdid the memorization," he said smiling.

Ellen came into the dining room and interrupted them. "My shadow is asleep in my bed!"

The family's surprise was overtaken with laughs. "Ellen, are you fully awake, dear?" the queen asked.

"Yes!" she declared indignantly. "I know when I see my shadow."

"You and the groundhog," Luke snickered.

Ellen shot him a warning glance. "If you don't believe me, come and see."

"Your turn," the king told the queen.

The queen sighed and got up from the table to accompany her daughter.

Once in Ellen's bedchamber, the queen said, "I see your bed is unmade, but I don't see your shadow. Do you?" she asked, looking worried.

"No," Ellen sighed.

"Ellen, you've been reading that poem night and day. It's no wonder you're seeing things when you're tired," the queen explained.

"I guess you're right," Ellen admitted. "How could my shadow be sleeping in my bed?" she giggled.

The queen laughed too. "Let's go have breakfast, shall we?" She put her arm around her daughter and pulled her close. Then the two returned to the dining room and reported that the shadow was gone.

"That's wonderful news!" the king declared. "I believe I'll celebrate by having more bacon and eggs," he said, grinning.

"By gum, I've got the answer!" the family heard someone call from the kitchen.

Luke's eyes grew wide. "They want my bacon, slice by slice, to sell at a tremendous price!" he said along with the voice in the kitchen. "There's a pig in there," he said, trembling.

"Nonsense!" the king declared. "Cook is just repeating your poem as she makes breakfast."

"It doesn't sound like Cook," Kirk said, looking just as unnerved as Luke.

The family heard a scream coming from the kitchen. Then a terrified Cook emerged. "There's a—a—"

"A pig?" Luke suggested.

31

Cook nodded rapidly and ran from the room in a panic.

The queen jumped onto her chair, screaming. "Do something!" she ordered her husband.

"Calm down, everyone. There is a reasonable explanation for this, I'm sure," the king insisted.

The door to the kitchen swung open and a pig walked into the room on two feet. He declared, "They want my tender juicy chops to put in all the butchers' shops!" He continued to walk and speak despite the king's commands.

The king quickly ushered his family out of the room. "What are we going to do?" the queen asked. She was nearly hysterical.

Ellen was crying. "Is he going to eat us, Father?" she asked.

"I'm going to call Animal Control right now. He is not going to eat us, all right?" the king tried to reassure them. His family nodded, hoping he was right.

While they waited for Animal Control, the king said they had to make their way to the library. "Good idea! He probably can't find us there," the queen said.

"Do pigs have a good sense of smell?" Luke asked. "If they do, he can probably find us there too." This suggestion began a fresh round of fearful exclamations.

"Pigs do have a good sense of smell, but they can't see very well," Kirk said. "Maybe we can trap him if he follows us to the library."

"We're going to leave his capture up to the experts, all right?" the king said, leaving no room for further discussion. "I want to get to the library to read *The Guidebook to Grammar Galaxy*. I think I know what's happening here."

Once in the library, the king retrieved the guidebook and asked Kirk to read the section on personification.

Personification
Personification is a literary device used to make stories or poems more interesting. It is giving human qualities to an animal or object. For example, animals or plants may speak, clouds may be angry, or stars may sing.

"My poem, 'The Raven', used personification," Kirk said, reflecting on what he'd read.

"Mine, too," Ellen said.

"We know mine did!" Luke exclaimed.

"But why did everything that was personified in our poems come to life?" Kirk asked.

"That's what we need to find out," the king said. "Screen, please give me a status update on planet Composition."

"Certainly, Your Majesty," Screen replied. After a moment, Screen played a video of a speech.

A man with the title of Chair of the Department of Rights stood at a podium. He read from a scroll he was holding. "By order of the king of Grammar Galaxy, animals, plants, and objects in this galaxy will no longer be second-class citizens. They're people too. You are hereby granted all the rights and privileges thereof. Everything that has been written about you is no longer just the stuff of dreams. The dream begins today!"

The king was astonished, then angry, then worried. "Kirk, Luke, and Ellen, I won't lie to you. This is a terrifying situation. If everything that has ever been personified lives out their script, we're in trouble. I'm going to put a stop to this ridiculous order, but it's going to take time. In the meantime, I need the three of you to send out a mission. We must find stories and poems that have personification, so we can put them in quarantine. If we don't, a hungry pig is the least of our worries."

The three English children worked on a personification mission and made plans to travel to planet Composition. While they were working, Animal Control reported that they had the pig in a cage in the back of their truck. The queen went to find Cook to tell her.

What does *erratic* mean?

What is personification?

Why was the king so worried about stories and poems with personification?

Chapter 6

"What has Mr. Wordagi been working on with you children?" the king asked one Saturday morning.

"We have been studying poetry," Ellen answered.

"We've been studying Shakespeare too," Luke added.

"Oh, wonderful!" the queen said. "I love Shakespeare!"

"Are you still doing copywork?" the king asked. When the children nodded, he seemed pleased.

"Remind me again why copywork is important," Luke said sighing.

"Copywork will help you improve your writing skills, including spelling, grammar, and punctuation," the king explained.

"I don't see how writing 'Juliet is the sun' is going to help me become a good writer," Luke complained. "That's just weird." As he finished speaking, Ellen pointed out the window, her eyes wide.

"I remember that line from playing Romeo," Kirk added. "I agree. It's weird."

"Look! Look! The sun looks like a person." Ellen said, pointing out the window. Her family peered out the window but could not see what Ellen was so excited about. "It was right there. The sun had a face!"

Kirk and Luke stifled a laugh. "The sun is really bright this morning," the king said. "It's normal to see things when you are staring directly at the sun."

"Yes dear, don't stare directly at the sun or you'll damage your eyes," the queen said.

Ellen rubbed her eyes and squinted at the sun again. "I don't see it now."

"Oh good. I was worried" the queen said.

"What are you three doing today?" the king asked his children, changing the subject.

"I have to decide if I'm going to be on the robotics team this year," Kirk said. "Today is the deadline for signing up."

Suddenly Kirk found himself at a fork in the road. One fork was wide and the other was narrow. Kirk looked around wildly, trying to get his **bearings**. "Where am I?" he asked himself. He closed his eyes and counted to 10, hoping that when he opened them, he would be back with his family. "One, two, three...," Kirk began. He couldn't wait until ten to open his eyes. When he did open them, he saw his family as he'd hoped.

★ ★ ★ ★ ★ ★ ★ ★ ★ ★

bearings – *directions*

angst – *worry*

diverged – *separated*

★ ★ ★ ★ ★ ★ ★ ★ ★ ★

"Kirk, you all right? " the queen asked, **angst** apparent on her face. "We were talking to you and you weren't answering us."

"Two roads **diverged** in a wood, and I, I took the one less traveled by," Kirk whispered.

"I love that poem! " the queen exclaimed.

"I like it too, " Kirk began. "But I just experienced it. "

"Oh, you mean trying to decide on the robotics team? " the queen asked.

"Yes. But I mean I really experienced it, " Kirk insisted.

"We understand, Kirk," the king said reassuringly. "These are challenging decisions. You don't know if you will regret your choice or not. Don't worry. If you don't participate on the team this year and you regret it, you can join next year, correct?"

"Yes, I could join next year. But something weird is happening," Kirk explained.

"Yes, you're growing up!" the queen said tearfully. The king patted her on the arm.

"You certainly are growing up, Kirk. No matter what you decide, we are here for you," the king said with as much emotion as his wife.

"That means a lot to me," Kirk said. It was obvious he wasn't going to get them to understand that he had literally been at a fork in the road. Hadn't he? Maybe he was really worried about making the wrong decision. He had copied Robert Frost's "Stopping by Woods on a Snowy Evening" many times. That's probably all it was. He decided to relax about it. "I'm going to go over to Leo's house to talk about it. If he plans to be on the team, I will probably do it too."

"That's a good idea, Kirk," the king said.
The queen stood and spoke loudly.

"Come, gentle night; come, loving, black-browed night;
Give me my king; and, when I shall die,
Take him and cut him out in little stars,
And he will make the face of heaven so fine
That all the world will be in love with night..."

That's from Romeo and Juliet, Kirk thought. He was still wondering why his mother was quoting from the play when his father stood and called out,

"See how she leans her cheek upon her hand.
O, that I were a glove upon that hand
That I might touch that cheek!"

"That's so romantic!" Ellen said.
Cook entered the room and paused dramatically before speaking.

"Find them out whose names are written here! It is written, that the shoemaker should meddle with his yard, and the tailor with his last, the fisher with his pencil, and the painter with his nets; but I am sent to find those persons whose names are here writ, and can never find what names the writing person hath here writ. I must to the learned.--In good time."

Kirk's eyes grew wide with understanding. "All the world's a stage, and all the men and women merely players," he said. "That's Shakespeare too. Father, Mother, listen to me. Something's wrong! Some of what we have been copying for Mr. Wordagi is coming to life. Ellen, you *did* see a face in the sun. I bet it was Juliet! I saw the road less traveled by. And now you are all being actors on a stage!"

Cook realized where she was and rushed back to the kitchen in embarrassment. The king frowned. "Why was I quoting from *Romeo and Juliet?*"

"Because you're a romantic?" the queen asked hopefully.
"I'd love to say yes, but I think Kirk is right. Something is wrong in the galaxy. What do these things have in common? It's not personification. 'Juliet is the sun,'" he said, thinking aloud. "I've got it!" he exclaimed after a few minutes of pacing. He called for *The*

Guidebook to Grammar Galaxy to be brought to him. He read the entry on similes and metaphors to his family when it arrived.

Similes and Metaphors
Similes and metaphors are comparisons that are used in stories and poems. These comparisons or analogies help readers form pictures in their minds. **Similes** typically compare one common feature using the word *like* or *as*. For example, *Her hands were as cold as ice.* **Metaphor** is a direct comparison that does not use the words *like* or *as*. For example, *Her hands were ice.* An entire story or poem can be a metaphor.

"'Stopping by Woods on a Snowy Evening' is a metaphor. He didn't really come to two roads. He had to make a decision. I understand now!" Kirk exclaimed. "But we still have a problem. It seems like the metaphors and not the similes are coming to life. Why?"

The king responded by asking Screen about any unusual activity in Analogy Province on planet Composition.

"Nothing in the news, Your Majesty," Screen reported.

"Do you want us to go check it out?" Luke asked hopefully.

"Yes. Some of these metaphors could be very dangerous for our planet if they were to become reality," the king said.

"Yes, like love is a –," Ellen began before being shushed. "Sorry," she apologized.

The three English children used the space porter to travel to Analogy Province. Once there, they alerted Grammar Patrol to the reason for their visit. An official accompanied them to one of the streets where metaphors resided. The group knocked on several doors and got no response.

"Where could they be?" Ellen asked.

They made their way to a neighboring street and knocked on a door. A simile answered and was unable to answer their questions. But it indicated that they should follow. The simile led them to a courthouse.

"Are they in legal trouble?" Kirk wondered aloud.

The official suggested they go inside. Peeking inside several courtrooms told them that many similes and metaphors were there.

"What are they doing here?" Kirk asked.

"It looks like jury duty," the official said.

"Does that explain all the strange things happening on planet English?" Luke asked.

Kirk took a moment to explain what had been happening to the Grammar Patrol official. He nodded. "They have to be sworn in as jurors. They have to promise to tell the truth," he explained.

"So now metaphors are considered truth," Ellen concluded.

"One guess who is behind all these similes and metaphors being called for jury duty," Luke said sarcastically.

"The Gremlin," Kirk and Ellen answered.

"Thanks so much for your help," Kirk told the official. "We have to get back and send out a mission to the guardians. If we can get you a list of metaphors, can you do anything to get them excused as jurors?"

"I should be able to object to them being sworn to tell the truth," he said.

"Great. We'll let the king know how helpful you've been," Kirk said.

The three of them got to work on a mission called "Similes and Metaphors" as soon as they returned. They reported their findings to their father.

What does *diverged* mean?

What's the difference between a simile and metaphor?

Why were the king, queen, and cook quoting from Shakespeare?

Chapter 7

Cook was in a tizzy. She and her staff were working to prepare corned beef and cabbage for a visiting **dignitary**. The king of planet Ireland himself and his **entourage** would be arriving that very afternoon. Cook had no idea if her meal would please their guests, so she was terribly anxious.

The rest of the household staff were also scurrying about, making sure the castle was prepared for overnight guests. The children, too, were busy getting ready to greet the visiting royal family. They had been assured that the family was fluent in English. Still, they had practiced a few Irish phrases to be polite.

The children were not surprised that their mother was anxiously barking orders at them. They knew she was afraid of being embarrassed in front of her guests. They tried to obey her promptly, so she wouldn't be upset.

"Let me see you," she said, fussing with their clothing and hair.

"They have a daughter my age, right, Mother?" Ellen asked.

"Yes, they do! And a son Kirk's age," the queen answered.

"Aw, it's no fair that I won't have anyone to—" Luke began. The queen warned him not to continue with a **scathing** look. "It will be fun," he said apologetically.

★ ★ ★ ★ ★ ★ ★ ★ ★ ★

scathing – *harsh*

★ ★ ★ ★ ★ ★ ★ ★ ★ ★

"Yes, it's all going to go smoothly or else," the queen insisted.

The king and the butler interrupted and announced that their guests had arrived. The family moved to the drawing room to greet them.

The king stepped forward first to shake the hand of the Irish king. His visitor smiled warmly and had a firm grip. The king was sure they would get along splendidly.

The queen air kissed the visiting queen near both cheeks. She hoped that was appropriate. Her fellow queen also smiled warmly, reassuring the English queen that the visit would go well.

Sean and Sophie, the couple's children, were also very cordial with the English kids. Kirk and Ellen were relieved.

The king suggested the visiting royal family be shown to their quarters where they could freshen up after their travels. After they were ready, he said he would be glad to give them a tour of the castle and grounds. The children especially seemed enthusiastic about this.

Their visitors were most impressed by the royal gardens. They said they planned to make some changes to their own gardens as a result. The king was flattered.

The queen of planet Irish also complimented her hostess on her decorating choices for the castle. The English queen blushed with pleasure. The visit was going so well.

The queen introduced her Irish counterpart to Cook who nervously shifted from foot to foot. The queen bragged about her cooking skill. She explained that Cook was making a traditional Irish dish for them.

The Irish queen graciously thanked her and said, "I hope you'll make some traditional English fare as well. I'm looking forward to it."

Cook was so relieved, she nearly collapsed. "It would be a pleasure, Your Highness!" she gushed after collecting herself.

At dinner that evening, Cook couldn't help but watch to see their guests' reaction to the corned beef and cabbage she'd prepared. She was so pleased when she saw they were enjoying it.

"How often do you have this dish at home?" the queen asked.

The Irish queen hesitated. "I don't believe we've ever had it, have we, dear?" she asked her husband.

"No, but I love it!" her husband exclaimed between bites.

Sean and Sophie nodded appreciatively.

The queen wondered how they could never have had a traditional Irish dish but said nothing.

After dinner, the king suggested they move to the sitting room. "We would love to learn more about your culture," the king said. His family nodded in agreement. "Tell us some things you've noticed that are different on planet Irish."

The Irish royal family began shyly at first to describe some differences they had noticed. The more the Irish family talked, the more their planetary pride was obvious. But they graciously praised their host planet as well.

"We would love for you to share a traditional English story with our children," the Irish king said.

"What a marvelous idea," the English king said. "Luke, you've gotten so good at telling stories. Why don't you tell them an English story?"

Luke's eyes grew wide. "Uh, an English story?"

"Yes, one of your favorites," his father said, encouraging him.

"Hm," Luke said, panicking. He knew some stories, but which were English? He did not want to be embarrassed in front of their guests by choosing a story they already knew. "I need to think of the best one to share," he said quickly. "Sophie or Sean could share an Irish story while I'm thinking. I would also love to hear a limerick," Luke said.

Sean and Sophie stared at one another and then at their parents. "We don't know any limericks," they said, trying not to offend Luke.

"Oh, okay. How about an Irish story then?" Luke asked.

41

The two Irish children seemed just as flustered as Luke in trying to think of one.

The English and Irish kings exchanged smiles. "I think we can help," the English king said. He called for *The Guidebook to Grammar Galaxy* to be brought to him. He read the entry on world literature.

World Literature
People have always told stories. Stories help us to learn more about others' culture and traditions and to celebrate our own. A story from another culture may not be well understood without knowing the beliefs and values of that culture.
The same story may be told around the world but with cultural differences. For example, there are more than 1500 versions of Cinderella – more than any other folktale. The original version was Chinese, which may explain why Cinderella had small feet. The English version is called *Tattercoats*. The Irish version, *The Irish Cinderlad,* has a male hero.

"I never thought of Cinderlad as an Irish story," Sophie said.

"I didn't think of Tattercoats as English either," Ellen agreed.

"It's like our two planets – similar, yet different," Kirk concluded.

"Indeed it is, Kirk. Through world stories, we see how much alike we are, yet also discover what makes us unique," the English king said. "Now I want to read to you children about limericks."

Limericks
A limerick is a five-line poem using the rhyming scheme *aabba*. The last words of lines 1, 2, and 5 rhyme as do the last words of lines 3 and 4. The rhythm of the poem includes three beats in the first, second, and fifth lines. It includes two beats in the third and fourth lines. The words or syllables that form the beats (or are emphasized) are in bold in the following limerick:
There **was** an old **man** of Pe**ru** Who **dreamt** he was **eat**ing his **shoe**. He **woke** in the **night**, With a **terr**ible **fright**, And **found** it was **perfect**ly **true**.

The origin of limericks is uncertain. But they appeared in British and Irish literature in the 1800s. British poet Edward Lear made limericks popular.

"So limericks are both English and Irish?" Luke asked.

"They are," his father agreed.

"It would be fun to write one," Sean said. Luke readily agreed.

"I would like to read Tattercoats," Sophie said.

"And I would like to read Cinderlad," Ellen said.

"Father, would it be rude to ask Sean and Sophie to help us write a mission during their stay? I imagine the guardians don't know any more about world literature or limericks than we do," Kirk said.

"That's entirely up to them," the king said, though it was clear he was pleased with the idea. The Irish king also smiled approvingly.

"We would love to help, wouldn't we, Sean?" Sophie said. Sean agreed, and the five royal children went to the library. They worked on a mission they called "Limericks and World Literature."

What does *scathing* mean in the story?

How many lines are in a limerick?

What dish did the queen and Cook assume the Irish family was used to eating?

Unit II: Adventures in Spelling & Vocabulary

Chapter 8

Luke awoke much earlier than normal. He was beaming when he found his father in the sunroom. "It's today! Finally, we get to see the total solar eclipse."

His father grinned. It pleased him to see his son so excited. "Do you have your eclipse glasses ready to go?" he asked.

Luke nodded. "Have you ever seen a total solar eclipse, Father?" he asked.

"I have. We traveled to see it when I was about your age. But there hasn't been a total eclipse visible from our city for 500 years. And I'm not that old," he said, chuckling.

Luke laughed too. "Do you think I should wake Kirk and Ellen?" he asked.

The king checked the time on the screen. "No, Luke. Let's let them sleep a little longer. We don't want them to be crabby." He smiled at his son's enthusiasm.

Luke agreed but was restless. His father asked him questions to keep him occupied. "Have you been reading about the eclipse?"

When Luke nodded, the king asked him to explain the difference between a lunar and a solar eclipse. "In a lunar eclipse, our planet passes between the moon and the sun. The shadow of our planet hides the moon from view. In a solar eclipse, the moon passes between our planet and the sun, blocking the sun from view."

"Very good, Luke! And tell me, why do we need to wear glasses today?"

"Because staring at the sun is dangerous for our eyes, even if it's partially blocked. I read that when the sun is totally blocked, we can take our glasses off," Luke answered.

"That will only be for a minute or two," the king said.

"One minute, fifty-three seconds," Luke said **assuredly**.

"Aha! You really have been reading," the king said, chuckling.

The two continued to talk about the eclipse. Eventually, they were called to breakfast, and the rest of the family joined them.

★ ★ ★ ★ ★ ★ ★ ★ ★ ★

assuredly – *confidently*

festive – *celebratory*

★ ★ ★ ★ ★ ★ ★ ★ ★ ★

Kirk and Ellen spoke animatedly about the day ahead. "It's going to be a big party, isn't it, Mother?" she asked.

"Yes, dear. Very exciting! Our friends will be there," the queen answered. "And we will have a picnic lunch that Cook has prepared."

Cook overheard them and opened the kitchen door a crack to say, "You're going to have moon pies for dessert." She seemed pleased with herself.

"What are moon pies?" Luke asked.

"I imagine we'll find out!" the queen replied.

Later that morning, the family and their dog, Comet, took the royal carriage to a public park. Thousands of people had already gathered there. There were picnic blankets, video cameras, and kids with eclipse glasses, who were running around the open area of the park. A band was playing in the auditorium, adding to the **festive** atmosphere.

Luke's eyes were wide as he took in the sight. He withdrew his communicator and checked the time. "We have an hour to eat and get ready for the total eclipse," he reminded them.

Ellen and the queen laid out the picnic supplies, while the boys and Comet went with their father to the stables. Their horses would be cared for there until the eclipse was over.

The royal family thoroughly enjoyed their picnic lunch and the moon pies. She had also packed a large bone to keep Comet busy during the eclipse. They promised to thank Cook when they returned to the castle.

Kirk set up his camera and solar filter and began filming at the beginning of the eclipse. People clapped and cheered when it started. Then they became strangely quiet when the sun was completely blocked. Luke removed his glasses and checked the temperature with his communicator. "In the dark—, the thermo— shows it's cooler without the sun's rays," he said.

Kirk nodded, thinking. "Herodotus said that a solar eclipse stopped a war between the Lydians and the Medes. They thought the eclipse was a sign to make peace."

46

"I can see why," the king said. The crowd was in awe and seemed very much at peace until the sun began to appear once again. They seemed reluctant to **disperse** when it was over.

★ ★ ★ ★ ★ ★ ★ ★ ★ ★

disperse– *scatter*

★ ★ ★ ★ ★ ★ ★ ★ ★ ★

"Did you get a good video, Kirk?" Luke asked.

"I don't know. Let's watch it," he said. When the two had finished watching it, Kirk said, "Not as incredible as seeing it in person, is it?"

Luke had to agree. Comet and the two boys went with their father to retrieve the carriage. Ellen and the queen cleaned up the picnic lunch and said goodbye to their friends.

Back at the castle, Kirk had Screen search for videos of the eclipse. He found one that was so impressive, he went to find his father and have him view it. "You have to see this video. It's a close-up view shot with a … with a … You know, it was made with a device that allows you to see things far away," he said.

"Oh, you mean a … a … Oh good grammar, it's a … It's a device you use to see things far away," the king said, getting frustrated.

"Right, you know what I mean. He used a different filter for viewing eclipses than I did," Kirk explained.

"I want to see it. Hopefully, the word will come to me then," the king said.

The king agreed that the video was spectacular. He tried to say the word that he couldn't recall earlier but still wasn't able to. "This is just —sense that I can't think of the word. I mean, it's silli—. Ack! It's —possible for me to say it," he stammered. His eyes grew wide with alarm. "Kirk, something is wrong."

"Hm. I noticed Luke used the word thermo for thermo— in the park. Whoops! I can't say the word either. I thought Luke was just trying to be cool. Could the eclipse have caused a problem on planet Vocabulary?" Kirk asked.

"It's possible the words were frightened, but planet Vocabulary wasn't in the path of the total eclipse. I have a bad feeling that this predica—, predica—, problem is the Gremlin's doing. We were all distracted by the eclipse. It was the perfect time to attack," the king said, beginning to pace with worry.

"It seems that we are only missing parts of words," Kirk said. "Except I can't say the name of the device that is used to see things in space."

The king sighed. "This has all the markings of a computer virus, Kirk. Some prefixes, suffixes, and root words are missing."

"Do you think Prefix and Suffix worked together on this attack?" Kirk asked.

"I can't think of another explanation. We need to check the Word Ancestry site. I think those two may have hacked the site and deleted some root words. If I'm right, we will need to have our programmer recover backup files."

Kirk agreed and went with his father to meet with their head programmer. He gave the two of them the bad news. He was able to identify which prefixes, suffixes, and root words had been affected by what he called the Eclipse Virus. But all the information about these word parts would have to be entered into the system manually.

Kirk turned to his father. "We're going to need the guardians' help," he said.

"Definitely," his father agreed.

Kirk and the king went to inform the rest of the family of the situation.

"Prefixes are at the beginnings of words and suffixes are at the end, right?" Luke asked.

"Right," the king said.

"And root words are what the prefixes and suffixes are added to," Ellen added. "Knowing the meanings of these word parts expands our vocabulary."

"You're also right," the king said, proud of his children.

Kirk showed them a list of missing parts and definitions because he still couldn't say them.

Prefixes	Definition	Examples
non-, in-, im-	not	nonsense, incorrect, impossible
over-	too much, above	overdone, overhead
de-	reduce, away from	decrease, defeat
tele-	far away, distant	telephone, television
bi-	two	bicycle
tri-	three	tricycle

quad-	four	quadrant
oct-	eight	octopus

Suffixes	Definition	Examples
-or	one who does	survivor, conductor
-tion	act, state, result of	concentration, motion
-al, -ial	related to, characterized by	regional, managerial
-ness	condition, state of	happiness, darkness
-ment	act, process	commitment, deployment
-en	made of, to make	woolen, strengthen

Roots	Definition	Examples
scope	see	microscope, telescope
rupt	break, burst	bankrupt, disrupt
terr	land	terrace, territory
tract	pull, drag	traction, tractor
meter, metr	measure	thermometer, metric

After reading the list, Luke said, "We need to send out an Eclipse mission right away!"

Kirk agreed but suggested they call it "Prefixes, Suffixes, and Root Words" to keep the guardians from being confused.

What does *disperse* mean?

What word (that means an instrument for viewing objects far away) couldn't Kirk and the king say?

What is the difference between a prefix and a suffix?

Chapter 9

The queen couldn't stop talking about her book club gathering that evening. Her friends would be joining her at the castle for the first meeting. They planned to choose the books they would read for the first half of the year. Each participant was to have a list of five books she wanted to read.

The queen had been talking to the head librarian and reading reviews of best-selling books to make her list. She was hoping to have a list of both classics and contemporary books. She didn't know what her friends would think of reading classics. She was nervous about her suggestions, but that wasn't all. She was also nervous about the refreshments. She would be serving tea and crumpets. Mints and nuts would also be available. She was nervous about the room. She had chosen to have the meeting in the parlor. She hoped it was cozy and private enough for the meeting. She wanted her friends to feel free to speak.

The truth was, she was also nervous about having so many ladies over. She was sometimes lonely being the queen. She wondered if her friends didn't call her as often as she would like because of her status. She hoped that tonight would break through any awkwardness and would show them that she was a woman just like them.

She didn't share all of this with her family, of course, but they could sense her nervousness. Ellen asked what she could do to help and the queen nearly burst into tears of gratitude. The queen asked Ellen's opinion about which tea set to use. The queen agreed with her choice and went to make sure it was clean and ready for her guests.

The queen had changed outfits numerous times. She didn't want to look too dressy, yet she wanted to look classy. The king quickly grew weary of giving his opinion, so Ellen stepped in to help her choose. "It's going to be so much fun, Mother," she said. "Don't worry."

"Yes, yes, you're right. I should be focusing on making my guests feel welcome, shouldn't I?" She didn't wait for Ellen to agree, but took some deep breaths and smiled.

She seemed to relax as soon as the first guest arrived. The queen noted with relief that her outfit was about the same level of dressiness as her own. She hugged her guest and Ellen **conducted** her to the parlor. The queen kept busy welcoming everyone who arrived. She was thrilled that each guest expressed her excitement about the book club. "It's like Grammar Girls for grown-ups!" one guest exclaimed.

★ ★ ★ ★ ★ ★ ★ ★ ★ ★

conducted – *escorted*

discombobulated – *confused*

★ ★ ★ ★ ★ ★ ★ ★ ★ ★

"Indeed!" the queen agreed, laughing heartily.

When everyone was in the parlor, the queen went in and announced that they would be starting with tea and crumpets. The ladies murmured their approval. "Please, set down and we'll begin."

A couple of women frowned and wondered if they had heard her wrong, then decided that they had. A server appeared with the teapot and the queen remembered that she wanted to tell them its story.

"Ladies, can I tell you about this teapot?" she asked, rising to her feet. The queen noticed two of her friends frowning and she was **discombobulated**. She stuttered, wondering if they thought she was boring already. "Uh, um...this teapot belonged to my great, great grandmother. She would raise up every morning and have tea from it." She couldn't help but notice more frowns. She rushed to finish talking so she wouldn't be thought a chatterbox. "She was a writer herself."

The guests oohed and aahed and the queen was encouraged. "Yes, she wrote romance novels." The queen's countenance fell when she noticed some disapproving looks. "They're lovely stories, honestly," she said.

"Do you have them?" one kindly woman asked. "I'd love to read them."

The queen was so thankful for this encouragement, she nearly cried. "Yes, of course! I'd love to lend them to you. I know my grandmother would be thrilled to have them read."

The other ladies asked if they might borrow them when the first friend was finished and the queen was further relieved. "Now then," she continued. "Can we discuss our book selections?"

One woman retorted, "Of course we *can*." The queen was confused. Why had the attitude taken a negative turn again?

Shaking, the queen said so quietly it was almost a whisper. "Wonderful."

The ladies shared their list of books they would like to read and each book was discussed. The queen could tell that her guests were excited about the book club. She told herself she was being silly and **paranoid** about their reactions earlier.

★ ★ ★ ★ ★ ★ ★ ★ ★ ★

paranoid – *suspicious*

★ ★ ★ ★ ★ ★ ★ ★ ★ ★

"Thank you, ladies, for choosing such interesting books. I wish we could read them all. But alas, we will have to choose just five of them for our club. I have a list of the books on my tablet. You can vote for three of them by rising your hand. The five books with the most votes will be our reading list for this session."

The queen expected to see smiles after her explanation, but she saw shock instead. Were they unhappy with the way she was choosing books? Did they want to vote for more than three? She was so distressed that she decided to ignore their reaction and get the meeting over with. She read the name of each book quickly and ladies tentatively raised their hands to vote.

"All right," the queen said, stifling tears, "it looks as though we have our selections." She read them and noted with great confusion that the ladies seemed pleased.

She invited everyone to enjoy the crumpets. Many compliments to Cook were given, and the ladies seemed to be enjoying the conversation. But the queen rushed them. "I know you can't stay late, so I will see you next month," she said repeatedly. The guests understood they were being asked to leave and were bewildered.

They didn't say so, but each thought the queen was behaving strangely. After the queen had said good-night to all of the guests, the king appeared, all smiles. "How did it go? Did they love the crumpets? Did you agree on books?"

The queen dissolved into tears and ran off saying, "I'm going to lay down."

"Lay down?" the king repeated. *She must be upset to use the wrong verb*, he thought.

The king wanted to find out what had happened, so he followed after her. She was sobbing in their bed. "Darling, what on English has upset you so?" he asked tenderly.

The queen drew a long, ragged breath to answer. "They hate me." She cried louder.

"Hate you? How could they hate you?" the king asked, rubbing her back. "You're the best friend anyone could have."

The queen cried even more. "That's—that's not—what they think," she sobbed.

"Tell me what happened," the king said patiently.

"I don't know! That's the problem," she sniffled. "From the moment I asked them to set down, they were cool toward me."

"You asked them to set down?" the king asked. He tried to hide his surprise for fear of upsetting her more.

"Yes!" the queen answered angrily. "That's what you do for guests, isn't it?"

"Yes, of course," the king said apologetically. "It's just that *set* isn't the correct verb to use."

The queen sat up angrily. "You're going to correct my grammar at a time like this?"

"No, of course, I'm not! I was just saying it wasn't like you to use bad grammar," the king said.

"So now I didn't just make a mistake and all my grammar is bad? Can I please be left alone so I can lay down?" she pleaded.

"Of course," the king said. He patted her on the back. "I'm really sorry. I did not mean to upset you."

The queen didn't answer and the king left quietly. He thought his wife was just being overly sensitive until she used several of the wrong verbs at once. He suspected that her behavior surprised her friends and caused a misunderstanding. If he was right, the queen wasn't the only one making these mistakes.

He decided to talk to the children and check their language. He found them in the game room. "Oh good, Father, I was just about to come looking for you," Luke said. "Can we play a game before bed?"

"No. We have a crisis," he said sternly.

"Ellen told us Mother is upset and went to lay down," Kirk said.

The king grimaced. "Yes. I think that's because the Gremlin is up to his old tricks again. I want you to come to the library with me. We need to consult *The Guidebook to Grammar Galaxy*."

The children dutifully followed him and listened closely as he read them an entry on verb confusion.

Verb Confusion

The meaning of the verbs *lie/lay*, *sit/set*, *rise/raise*, and *can/may* are commonly confused. The difference between the first three verb pairs is similar: *Lie*, *sit*, and *rise* are intransitive verbs with no objects. *Lay*, *set*, and *raise* are transitive verbs that require an object of the action.

Some tricks to remember the difference are:
Lie = recline; lay = place. The word and its meaning have the same vowel sound.
A dog sits where you set his bowl.
You rise to raise your glass.

The past tense of these verbs can add to the confusion. See the chart below.

Present	Past
lie	lay
lay	laid
sit	sat
set	set
rise	rose
raise	raised

Can means to be able and *may* means to have permission. The game "Mother, May I?" can remind you that *may* means asking permission.

<u>Incorrect</u>

The cat laid down for a nap.	Raise up in protest.
Set yourself down for a rest.	Can I go over to my friend's house?

"Your mother has been confusing these verbs," the king explained.

"But the guidebook says it's common to confuse them," Kirk said.

"Right, but your mother doesn't confuse them," the king said.

"That rises another question: Why is Mother confusing the verbs?" Luke asked.

"Your Mother isn't the only one. The correct word is *rises*. Great grammar, now I'm doing it! We have to determine what the Gremlin has done to confuse these verbs," the king said. "Screen, give me a status report on Verb Village."

"Everything appears to be in order, Your Majesty," Screen reported.

"I was afraid of that. It's never a simple answer, is it?" he said, trying to contain his frustration. "What could the Gremlin have done to confuse these verbs? They're related words, but they're not identical." He thought for a moment and then became alarmed. "Could he have had them categorized as identical verbs? My guess is he has them living together as twins. You three are going to have to go to Verb Village and sit the record straight. Oh, you know what I mean."

Kirk, Luke, and Ellen drew up an action plan and worked with the king to create a mission called "Verb Confusion." As soon as they were finished, the king went to give the queen the good news that her book club friends did not hate her.

What does *paranoid* mean?

How can you remember the difference between *lie* and *lay*?

Why was the queen confusing her verbs?

Chapter 10

The king eagerly opened his *Universal Geographic* magazine. He had been waiting for a promised article about the first around-the-universe trip. He showed the cover photo to his family and said he would read the article to them.

Fifteen months ago, Mr. Escapade went on a trip that had never been tried before. He got into his space shuttle, not knowing if he would live. He did, of course.

Mr. Escapade said he was happy to be back home but liked seeing the other galaxies around the universe.

When I asked him to describe them, he said they were big groups of stars and planets.

Once a light on the control panel showed that he was out of fuel. He was scared until he found out the light was wrong.

I asked him how he passed the time between visits to other galaxies. He said he read a lot. He also took a lot of pictures.

Mr. Escapade said the people of math, science, and art galaxies were very nice. They helped him any way they could. They gave him great gifts to take back with him.

When I asked him to describe the whole trip, he said, "Good." He told me he plans to rest, though he may take another trip sometime soon.

"I can't believe it!" the king exclaimed.

"I know. He traveled around the universe by himself and made it back safely," the queen enthused.

"That's not what I mean," the king said.

"Didn't you help fund the trip, Father?" Kirk asked. "He didn't thank you, did he?"

"Yes, I did help fund the trip, but his not mentioning me isn't what I can't believe," the king explained.

"What is it then, dear?" the queen asked.

"The writing in the article is atrocious!" the king exclaimed.

Luke took the magazine from his father. "Is it full of spelling errors?" he asked.

"No," the king began before being questioned by Kirk.

"Grammar errors again?" Kirk asked.

"No to that too. I don't know how an around-the-universe trip can be that boring to read about," the king answered.

"Hm. It wasn't as exciting as I was expecting either," Kirk said. The rest of the royal family had to agree.

"Are you going to complain to the editor of the magazine?" the queen asked.

"I would like to, but I can't keep complaining to our editors."

"Right. It isn't good manners to complain all the time," the queen agreed.

"I have an idea," the king said, cheering up. "I'm going to invite Mr. Escapade to the castle for a visit."

"That's a splendid idea," the queen said. "Then you can hear for yourself about the trip."

"Right, but I'm going to invite another guest too—Walter Word, the best travel journalist I know. It's true that *Universal Geographic* got the scoop on the story, but there is so much more to be said. Walter can bring the story to life for everyone."

"I'm so pleased. The children will get to meet an explorer and a top journalist," the queen said.

A few weeks later, the planned visit took place. The entire family was entranced by Mr. Escapade's description of his trip. They were on the edge of their seats as he talked about the time the ship's fuel warning light came on. They listened with rapt attention as he **amused** them with funny and surprising facts about the people of other galaxies.

★ ★ ★ ★ ★ ★ ★ ★ ★ ★

amused – *entertained*

★ ★ ★ ★ ★ ★ ★ ★ ★ ★

After dinner, Mr. Escapade showed the group a slideshow of the trip, including some shots of him in the ship. He apologized for his appearance. "I wasn't able to bathe while on ship. The aroma wasn't delightful, even for me," he joked. Walter Word took **copious** notes as he spoke. The king was so pleased. Even though he had the privilege of speaking with the explorer personally, he wanted everyone in the galaxy to share the experience. Walter would make that happen with his powerful writing.

★ ★ ★ ★ ★ ★ ★ ★ ★ ★

copious – *abundant*

★ ★ ★ ★ ★ ★ ★ ★ ★ ★

The two guests graciously thanked their hosts and promised to visit again soon.

In the days that followed, the king had to keep himself from pestering Walter about the article. He knew that a quality article took time. He wondered if the *Universal Geographic* article had been rushed and that was the problem with it.

When a copy of Walter's newly published article was finally brought to the king, he gathered everyone around to hear it. "This will be a treat!" he said. His family believed him after meeting both men responsible for the article.

I had the chance to meet Mr. Escapade a few weeks ago. By now, he is a man you all know. He took a trip around the universe in a one-man shuttle.

He said he was happy at the start of the trip but soon became scared. If anything happened, he was all alone.

Something did happen. His fuel light came on. He had no fuel. He thought he would die. He was scared. But the light was wrong, and he didn't die.

He went on to meet people from many different galaxies around our universe. They were different from us but nice. Some made him laugh. They gave him things to take home.

When I asked Mr. Escapade what he thought of the trip overall, he said it was very good. "Would he do it again?" I asked. He would. But

59

for now, he is going to rest.

My visit with Mr. Escapade made me want to go on an around-the-universe trip. How about you?

The king's cheeks grew red with anger. *Uh-oh*, Luke thought.

The queen noticed too. "Are you disappointed, dear?" she asked.

"Of course, I am! I expected so much more from Walter. He is an award-winning journalist. Mr. Escapade made the trip come to life for all of us who listened to him and this," he said pointing to the article, "is just awful!"

"Do you think your standards are too high?" the queen asked hesitantly.

"No, I don't!" the king roared. The question touched a nerve. He had been criticized for expecting too much many, many times.

The queen apologized, but the king said he needed time to calm down. The family encouraged him and after he left, they discussed the article.

"Did you think it was a bad article, Mother?" Ellen asked.

"Well, it wasn't as exciting as talking with Mr. Escapade himself. But what would be?" the queen answered. The children nodded to agree with her.

"May I see the article?" Kirk asked. His mother handed it to him. He read it over slowly. "You know what this reminds me of?"

"Charles Lindbergh's flight?" Luke asked.

"No, not the trip, the writing. Remember when WordBook was closing word accounts on planet Vocabulary when they weren't getting enough likes?" When his siblings and mother nodded, he continued. "We couldn't use some words. In this article and the first one in *Universal Geographic*, Mr. Escapade describes his trip as good. Yet he told us it was spectacular, awe-inspiring, and thrilling. He didn't say he was scared when the fuel light warning came on. He said he was terrified! Why did a talented writer like Walter Word use words like *good* and *scared* in his article?"

His three family members admitted they didn't know.

"I don't either, but I'm going to find out," Kirk said. Luke and Ellen joined him in walking to the castle library.

When they arrived, Kirk asked Screen for a status report on planet Vocabulary. Nothing unusual appeared, so Kirk asked for a list of articles about the planet, even if they weren't headlines.

He bypassed a headline about the weather and scanned an article about new words from the past year. Then he read about the Royal Fitness Program with great interest. He didn't remember hearing about the program.

By order of the king, the article said, strong words were not to be used in compositions until weak words improved their strength. The way for weak words to get stronger, according to the program's guidelines, was for them to be used more. The article included a photo of the words *good*, *bad*, and *went*, which appeared to be sweating with effort. Strong words were to be **secluded** until the weak words increased their strength.

★ ★ ★ ★ ★ ★ ★ ★ ★ ★

secluded – *removed*

★ ★ ★ ★ ★ ★ ★ ★ ★ ★

"That doesn't sound good," Ellen said.

"You mean it sounds like a disaster!" Luke exclaimed.

"Right. Let's see if the guidebook has any information on strong vocabulary words," Ellen suggested. When she found the entry, she read it for them.

Strong Vocabulary

A strong vocabulary includes words that are descriptive. Strong vocabulary words help readers and listeners form pictures in their minds. To create a strong vocabulary, replace weak vocabulary words like *good*, *great*, *bad*, *nice*, *scary*, *mad*, *went*, *pretty*, *big*, *little*, *happy*, *sad*, and *saw* with more descriptive options you find in a thesaurus. Review the chart of weak word alternatives. Note: not every alternative word is a good fit. Look up the precise meaning of alternative words.

Good	Bad	Scary	Went
incredible	horrible	terrifying	ambled
remarkable	dreadful	horrifying	cruised
amazing	awful	petrifying	dashed
terrific	despicable	unnerving	departed
superior	disgraceful	eerie	fled
fantastic	shameful	creepie	proceeded
excellent	atrocious	chilling	traveled

"The program that Father supposedly started will make everyone's vocabulary weaker, not stronger," Kirk said.

"Exactly. And that's why both articles about Mr. Escapade's trip weren't interesting to read," Ellen added.

The three found their father in his study and told explained the problem with the Royal Fitness Program. The king was both annoyed and relieved.

"I'm sure this is the Gremlin's doing," he said. His children had to agree. "I can get the fitness program canceled, but I will need you children to identify strong vocabulary words. We have to bring them home. I must admit, though, that I like the idea of a royal fitness program. Weak writing isn't just the result of strong words being relocated. Weak writing is the result of weak writers who don't give their vocabularies a workout."

"Do you mean we have to exercise before we write?" Luke asked.

The king laughed. "No, though exercise does promote blood flow to the brain which could help your creativity. What I mean is writers must do the work of editing. They need to use their thesaurus to find strong words. Then weak words should be replaced with strong words."

"We need to get to work, don't we, Father?" Kirk asked.

The king nodded and the three guardians created a mission they called "Strong Vocabulary."

What does *secluded* mean?

What are some of the weak words in the articles about the trip?

What writing tool do writers need to use to find strong vocabulary words?

Chapter II

"Luke, you misspelled *answer* here," the queen said, pointing to the tablet in front of her. Luke frowned. "And *prove* is misspelled, too."

Luke groaned. "Spelling is impossible to learn."

"What's this?" the king asked. He was reading his paper but overheard Luke's complaint about spelling. "Spelling is not impossible to learn. I would say color coordinating is impossible though." He smirked, and the queen laughed.

"You are probably right that color coordinating is impossible for you to learn. I've spent years trying to teach you to no **avail**," the queen said, grinning.

"I give up!" Luke exclaimed, ignoring his parents' **banter**. He started to walk away when his father stopped him.

"Luke, why are you so upset about this?"

"Why? Because no matter how hard I try, I still make spelling mistakes. Kirk and Ellen don't misspell words all the time. Why do I? I'm hopeless," Luke said, near tears.

The queen gasped. "Luke, don't say that! You are not hopeless. You've learned to spell many words that you used to misspell."

Luke hung his head. "I've learned to spell some words, but I still make mistakes all the time."

"Luke, maybe you have the wrong goal. You want to spell every word correctly. That's fine for Spelling Bee champions. But we just want you to keep learning. Make your goal to learn the spelling of as many words as you can. That's a better goal than never making a mistake," the king said.

Luke thought for a moment. "But what if I'm never as good a speller as Kirk or Ellen?"

"I'm never going to be as patient as your mother. Does that mean you don't love me as much as you love her?" the king asked.

"No."

"All right then. You and Kirk and Ellen have different strengths and weaknesses, but we love each of you," the king explained.

Luke sighed heavily. "I just wish I didn't even have to learn to spell. It's so hard. I hate it!"

"Luke, why don't you take a break," his mother suggested. "Our studies always seem easier when we come back to them with fresh eyes."

"I don't see how spelling will be any easier, but I'll gladly take a break," he said. He decided to take Comet outside for a walk. His parents agreed it was a wonderful idea.

When he left, the queen expressed her frustration at not being able to help him spell. "I've taught him how to spell phonetically and we've learned spelling rules," she said.

"Yes, dear, but some children will find spelling challenging even when taught spelling rules," the king said.

"Why?" the queen asked. "Could there be something wrong with his vision?"

"He's always passed vision screenings. Some people don't notice how words are spelled and have trouble remembering what letters represent."

The queen pointed out the sunroom window, where she had spotted Luke and Comet. Luke was **gesticulating** wildly and appeared to be very excited.

★ ★ ★ ★ ★ ★ ★ ★ ★ ★

gesticulating –*waving*

★ ★ ★ ★ ★ ★ ★ ★ ★ ★

"What's he doing?" the king asked.

"My guess is he has spotted a new bird. Yes, he is recording it," the queen noted.

"He is tracking birds?"

"Yes, he is studying ornithology and is trying to identify as many species as he can," the queen said.

"That's a wonderful hobby for him," the king said. "I haven't studied birds. I'll ask him about it to cheer him up."

"You're a great father," the queen said, pecking him on the cheek.

The king smiled appreciatively. "Only because I have you to keep me in line."

"Well, that's true," the queen said, laughing.

At dinner that evening, the king asked Luke about his birding. "What bird did you spot that you were so excited about?"

"It was a Red Crossbill! At first, I thought it was a Purple Finch. But when I got close enough, I could see that the top and bottom of the beak crossed like this," Luke said, demonstrating with his fingers. Their bill helps them eat the seeds in pine cones."

The rest of the family expressed interest in Luke's description. "Screen, can you show us a Red Crossbill?" Luke requested.

"Certainly, Your Highness," Screen answered. The family gushed over the bird and Luke was proud to have found it.

"How common is the Red Crossbill?" the king asked.

"It's a fairly common bird, but unless we pay attention to the bill that makes it different, we won't see it," Luke explained. "Before I started studying ornithology, I wouldn't have noticed it."

"That's interesting. I have to admit I wouldn't have noticed this bird unless you'd told me," the king said.

The queen told Luke she was proud of him for pursuing a new hobby. "But we do need to finish editing your paper tonight."

Luke groaned. "I don't know why I'm bothering to fix the spelling errors. I'll never learn."

The king was excited as he heard Luke complain. "Luke, I have an idea." He requested *The Guidebook to Grammar Galaxy* be brought to him. When it arrived, he read the entry on unusual spelling to the family.

Unusual Spellings

English orthography (spelling) is not unpredictable. Half of English words are spelled the way they sound. Another 36% of words have one sound with an unusual spelling – typically a vowel.

To learn unusual spellings, notice words that are not spelled the way you would predict. Write them down and then use a strategy for memorizing them.

For example, the word *Wednesday* includes a d and an e that aren't voiced. Highlight the d and e. Write the word *Wednesday* several times. Use a saying like "Nancy sits between Denise and Ellen on Wednesday" to remember that there is a d-n-e in the middle of the word.

"I understand that I need to look for words with unusual spellings. But I don't think I can remember them," Luke said, obviously discouraged.

"Do you remember the difference between a Purple Finch and a Red Crossbill?" the king asked.

"Of course. That's easy," Luke said.

"But you said that before you studied birds, you wouldn't have seen the difference," the king said.

"That's right," Luke agreed.

"Spelling is a lot like birding. You need to be on the lookout for words with unusual spellings just like you look for birds with unusual bills or markings," the king said, proud of himself.

"Hm. I hadn't thought of it that way," Luke said.

"Luke, you could keep track of the unusually spelled words you find, just like you do with birds. That could help you remember!" the queen said, excited by the idea.

"I don't know..." Luke said, unsure.

"You can do it, Luke!" Ellen said.

"You definitely can," Kirk added. "You know what I think would help?" he asked.

"Ice cream?" Luke suggested. Everyone laughed.

"No, I was thinking that we need to send out a mission. If you know our guardian friends are looking for unusual words too, it'll be fun for you," Kirk explained.

"You're not the only one who has a hard time with spelling. Some of my friends do too," Ellen said.

Luke smiled. "Mission accepted. Let's work on an Unusual Spelling mission, but after we have ice cream."

What does *banter* mean?

Why was Luke upset when editing his paper?

How is looking for unusual spellings like birding?

Chapter 12

"Kirk, when is your article for *Robotics Today* due?" the king asked. He stood outside Kirk's bedchamber.

"It isn't due until next week, but I submitted it today," Kirk said proudly.

"That's my boy! It always pays to be early," the king congratulated him. "What angle did you take with the article?"

"I was supposed to write about how today's robots are making it possible for people to use the analog approaches they're comfortable with. I wrote about a program I created for my robot that allows it to digitize text. As an example, I hand wrote my article. My robot digitized it and submitted it to the editor."

"I'm impressed! There are a lot of old-school writers who will love your program. I can't wait to read the article. Let me know when you hear from the editor."

"I will," Kirk said. He was pleased that his father seemed so proud of him.

The next day, Kirk seemed out of sorts at dinner. When his parents **persisted** in asking him about his mood, he **relented** and told them what was wrong. "I heard from the editor of *Robotics Today*."

★ ★ ★ ★ ★ ★ ★ ★ ★ ★

persisted – *continued*

relented – *gave in*

★ ★ ★ ★ ★ ★ ★ ★ ★ ★

"And?" his father prompted him.

"And there was a problem," Kirk said, sighing. "My program did turn my handwritten article into text. But my robot doesn't have a spell checker. So, my spelling errors were left in the article."

"*You* had spelling errors?" Luke asked in shock.

"You sound like the editor. He seemed surprised and disappointed," Kirk said. "I'm mad at myself that I didn't think to use a spell checker before I submitted it. I thought I was good at spelling."

"You *are* a good speller," the queen said.

"You are," the king agreed. "Are you sure your program was accurate? Perhaps your robot didn't read the letters accurately."

"That was my first thought. I checked, and everything was copied correctly," Kirk said.

"You didn't check that before you submitted the article?" the king asked.

"No," Kirk admitted.

"That wasn't wise, Kirk. We always need to review papers before turning them in," the king said.

"I know," Kirk said, agreeing.

"If the robot isn't at fault and Kirk is misspelling words, shouldn't we make sure everything is all right on planet Spelling?" Luke asked.

"That's a good idea, Luke," the king replied. He asked Screen for a status report on the planet. Screen could find nothing **amiss**.

★ ★ ★ ★ ★ ★ ★ ★ ★ ★

amiss – *wrong*

★ ★ ★ ★ ★ ★ ★ ★ ★ ★

"That doesn't mean the Gremlin isn't up to something," Luke said.

"You're right, Luke," his father agreed. "You three may need to go to the planet to check things out."

"I'm ready to go now," Luke said.

"Wait a minute," the queen interjected. "Kirk, may I see the article you submitted?"

"Sure. But why?" Kirk asked.

"I want to see which words were misspelled."

"Okay. It's embarrassing though." Kirk used his communicator to have the article sent to his mother's tablet.

The queen began reading the article. She murmured and nodded as she read. She read the entire article before she responded. By that time, Kirk was anxious.

"It's a very well-written article, Kirk," she began. I see the spelling errors too. But I don't think you three have to leave for planet Spelling. I don't think this is the Gremlin's fault."

"Are you saying Kirk is just bad at spelling like me?" Luke asked hopefully.

The queen stifled a laugh. "No. Kirk is good at spelling, but he misspelled some words that are commonly misspelled." Before Kirk could ask her to explain, she requested that *The Guidebook to Grammar Galaxy* be brought to her from the library.

Once it arrived, she read the article on commonly misspelled words.

Commonly Misspelled Words

The most commonly misspelled words according to the Oxford English Corpus are:

accommodate	achieve	across	aggressive	apparently
appearance	argument	assassination	basically	beginning
believe	bizarre	business	calendar	Caribbean
cemetery	colleague	coming	committee	completely
conscious	curiosity	definitely	dilemma	disappear
disappoint	ecstasy	embarrass	environment	existence
familiar	finally	fluorescent	foreign	foreseeable
forty	forward	friend	further	gist
glamorous	government	guard	happened	harass
honorary	idiosyncrasy	immediately	incidentally	independent
interrupt	irresistible	knowledge	liaison	lollipop
millennium	Neanderthal	necessary	noticeable	occasion
occurred	occurrence	pavilion	persistent	pharaoh
piece	politician	Portuguese	possession	preferred
propaganda	publicly	really	receive	referred
religious	remember	resistance	sense	separate
siege	successful	supersede	surprise	tattoo
tendency	therefore	threshold	tomorrow	tongue
truly	unforeseen	unfortunately	until	weird
wherever	which			

Use one or more spelling strategies to memorize the correct spellings of these words.

See also: Spelling Strategies

When the queen finished reading the entry, Kirk urged her to read the Spelling Strategies entry too.

Spelling Strategies

There are at least three ways that may help you to remember the spellings of commonly misspelled words.

First, consider the prefix, root word, and suffix of the word. For example, the word *unfortunately* is made up of the prefix *un-*, the suffixes *–ate* and *–ly*, and the root word *fortune*. When you know the rules for adding suffixes, you can put the word parts together correctly. The *e* in the root word *fortune* is dropped before adding the suffix *-ate*. This is because the suffix begins with a vowel. For the same reason, the word *coming* does not have an *e* because we usually drop it before adding *–ing*.

The second strategy is to look for words within the word. For example, the word *knowledge* has two words in it: *know* and *ledge*.

Third, make up a saying to help you remember a tricky spelling. The saying could be based on an acronym like "It's necessary to cut some services" to remember the spelling of *necessary*. The first letters of "cut some services" can remind you that there is one *c* and two *s*'s in the word. Or memorize a saying like "There are two m's, two t's, and two e's in committee." Use the same strategy for remembering several words with the same unique spelling. For example, remember "Her resistance to his appearance at the dance." All three main words end in *-ance*. Combine the second strategy with the third to remember how to spell *finally*. "Fin finally became my ally."

"I remember you teaching me how to spell *friend* with a saying," Luke exclaimed. "You said 'I am your friend to the end' because there's an *i* followed by the word *end*."

"Exactly, Luke," the queen said.

"I'm going to find all the misspelled words in my article and correct them," Kirk said.

"That's a wonderful idea," the queen said.

"I was spelling some of those words wrong, too, Kirk," Ellen admitted.

"And you know I was," Luke joked.

"I want to start using these strategies, so I won't forget how to spell these words," Kirk said. "It's like hacks for spelling."

"I think you should wait, Kirk," Luke said.

"Why would I wait?" Kirk said.

"Because I think we should send this out as a mission to the guardians first," Luke answered.

Kirk smiled. "You're right. I know for sure I'm not the only one who needs a way to remember to spell these words."

The three guardians got to work on a mission they called "Commonly Misspelled Words."

What does *amiss* mean?

Why did Kirk misspell some words in his article?

Have you misspelled any of the commonly misspelled words?

Chapter 13

The king was in a cheerful mood at breakfast. It was the day of the finals in the Galaxy Spelling Bee. He would be giving the winner the highly **coveted** trophy. He had the whole family accompany him every year.

★ ★ ★ ★ ★ ★ ★ ★ ★ ★

coveted – *desired*

★ ★ ★ ★ ★ ★ ★ ★ ★ ★

Luke seemed less than enthusiastic about attending. When his mother noticed, he complained, "I have never even heard of these words. How can these kids spell them? They must be freaks of nature."

The king tried not to laugh. "They are not born knowing how to spell, Luke. These students study many hours to be able to compete at this level."

"I can think of more fun things to do than study the dictionary," Luke said sourly.

"I know it's not how you like to spend your **leisure** time. But many students are passionate about improving their spelling and vocabulary skills," the king said. "I appreciate their hard work."

★ ★ ★ ★ ★ ★ ★ ★ ★ ★

leisure – *relaxation*

disingenuously – *dishonestly*

★ ★ ★ ★ ★ ★ ★ ★ ★ ★

"I don't know how they do it," Luke said, shaking his head.

"After today, perhaps you will," the king said. "I have arranged to have the winner and the winner's family join us for dinner this evening. You can ask all the questions of a spelling champion you'd like."

Luke could think of more exciting children to spend time with, but he knew he would be chastised for saying so. "That will be great," he said **disingenuously**. The king seemed irritated but said nothing.

That afternoon the royal family sat watching the finalists compete in the spelling bee. Everyone but Luke expressed appreciation and awe at the competitors' knowledge. He was annoyed that he had to watch spelling geniuses when spelling ordinary words was a challenge for him.

The winning word was *gesellschaft*. It seemed like it was from another planet. The girl who won was so excited. Her father hugged her and her mother cried. Luke guessed his mother would call them happy tears. The winner was beaming when the king handed her the trophy.

He felt funny as he watched her. He elbowed Kirk and asked, "Are you happy for her?"

"Of course!" he answered as he continued to applaud.

"I'm not."

"You're jealous, Luke. She worked very hard to win this competition. You should be happy for her," Kirk said.

Luke knew his brother was right. He forced himself to smile and clap and he felt a little better. He worried about how dinner would go, however.

75

The winner (her name was Leah), her parents, and her younger brother seemed thrilled to be riding in one of the king's hovercrafts to the castle. That made Luke feel a little guilty. He was able to do cool things like that all the time. He was a prince, after all.

When the party arrived at the castle, Cook had a feast prepared for them. She shook Leah's hand and told her how proud she was of her. She said she hoped Leah would enjoy the banquet as she deserved it for all her hard work.

Hm, Luke thought. *Cook has never seemed that proud of me. I wonder if she would make me a special feast if I won the spelling bee. That'll never happen*, he thought bitterly.

During the meal, Luke resented all the attention that was paid to Leah. "How does it feel to win? Are you surprised? Which words were you unsure of?" they asked. Even Leah's little brother seemed fascinating to his family. "What's it like to see your sister become spelling champion of the galaxy? Are you a speller too?"

Oh, come on! Luke wanted to scream. *It's just a stupid spelling bee,* he groused to himself.

During dinner, the king's assistant appeared. "I'm so sorry to interrupt, Your Majesty, but there is an urgent matter that requires your attention," he said.

"Excuse me," the king said, apologizing to his guests.

While he was gone, Luke silently sulked and thought of all the things he did well that were more important than spelling. He was so preoccupied that he didn't even enjoy the dessert the rest of those at the table raved about.

When the king returned to the table, the queen said she hoped it was nothing serious. "As a matter of fact, the issue concerns spelling," he said, smiling at Leah. "It seems that we have a number of foreign words who have taken refuge on planet Spelling. There is a group demanding that we change our English spelling rules to help the foreign words feel more comfortable."

"Are they all from the same planet?" Leah asked.

"No, they are from a number of different planets and I don't believe they needed to take refuge here. I suspect the Gremlin rounded them up, sent them, and is using them to make English spelling more complicated."

"*More* complicated?" Luke interjected without thinking. He blushed and looked down at his dessert.

"Yes, the English language has long been criticized for its spelling challenges," he said, smiling at Leah. He looked thoughtful for a moment and asked, "What would you do in my place? Would you change English spelling rules to make foreign words feel more comfortable?"

Leah smiled shyly. "I agree with you that it would make spelling more complicated. We learn spelling rules for foreign words that are part of English vocabulary when we prepare for the bee. It's manageable to learn them because they apply to a small pool of words. But if you changed the rules for English words without reason, spelling would prove to be impossible."

"Of course, you are right, Leah. Thank you for sharing your opinion with me," the king said.

"You know English spelling rules *and* foreign spelling rules?" Luke asked, aghast at the idea.

Leah laughed. "I don't know every foreign spelling rule. But I know enough of the rules or unique spellings to spell a lot of words."

"Obviously!" Kirk exclaimed.

"Leah, I am afraid I have not taught my children about foreign spellings. I'm going to have *The Guidebook to Grammar Galaxy* brought to us. Would you do us the honor of reading the entry on foreign words?" the king asked.

Leah agreed and read the entry for the group.

Foreign Words

Foreign words in the English language are also known as loanwords. The three languages that contribute the most loanwords are Latin, French, and German.

Latin Spelling Tips

The \$\overline{oo}$\ sound is usually spelled with a *u* as in *lucid* and *lunatic* when it follows a \d\, \j\, \l\, \r\, or \s\ sound. After other consonants, it sounds like \y$\overline{oo}$\ as in *refugee* or *bugle*.

Some Latin words spell the \s\ sound with sc, including *crescent*, *susceptible*, and *discipline*.

The letter *k* is rarely used in Latin words. Instead, words like *aquatic*, *canine*, and *corporal* are spelled with *c*.

French Spelling Tips

French usually spells \sh\ with *ch* as in *cachet*, *chagrin*, and *quiche*.

French words ending in the \äZH\ sound are spelled *age* as in *collage*, *barrage*, and *garage*.

A \k\ sound at the end of a word is often spelled with *que* as in *physique*, *mystique*, and *boutique*.

German Spelling Tips

The \k\ sound is spelled with *k* at the start of a word or syllable and is spelled with *ck* at the end. For example, *kitsch*, *kuchen*, *rucksack*.

The long *i* sound \ī\ is usually spelled *ei* as in *einkorn*, *eiderdown*, and *Fahrenheit*.

The \sh\ sound is usually spelled *sch* as in *schnauser*, *anschluss*, and *schottische*.

"So that's why you asked the origin of words during the competition," Kirk concluded.

"Exactly. I could at least make an educated guess," Leah said.

"You had to guess?" Luke asked.

Leah smiled at his surprise. "Every competitor has to guess at some words."

"I have to do that for almost every word," Luke joked. Everyone laughed. "I don't even know what a lot of those words mean!"

"We study the meaning of words and not just the spelling," Leah said.

"You must know a lot of words," Luke said as a compliment. Leah smiled.

"Father, I'm thinking the guardians should complete a mission on foreign words," Kirk said.

"That's a splendid idea. Leah, would you be willing to help these three create a mission?" the king asked. "I need to deal with the refugee words."

Leah seemed delighted to help. Her younger brother was excited about helping too.

What does *disingenuously* mean?

Why wouldn't it be a good idea to change English spelling to match foreign spelling rules?

Did Leah have every foreign spelling rule memorized?

Chapter 14

The royal English children were just as excited as their friends about their trip to the capital that morning. The king chuckled as he listened to their excited chatter.

The queen was joining them on the trip and was busy collecting the lunches Cook had prepared for them. She was excited to see her children's reaction to the Capitol building itself. It was full of one-of-a-kind paintings and historical **artifacts**. Their group had also arranged for an excellent tour guide, who would make the history and significance of the place come to life. The children would also be able to see words being capitalized.

★ ★ ★ ★ ★ ★ ★ ★ ★ ★

artifacts – *objects*

exemplary – *excellent*

derived – *taken from*

★ ★ ★ ★ ★ ★ ★ ★ ★ ★

For once, the queen didn't have to hurry the children along. They were eager to go to the space depot where they were meeting their group. They were eager to see their friends as was the queen.

The family wished the king farewell. He had committed himself to a game of golf with friends. He hadn't played in ages, so he was looking forward to it.

The trip on the shuttle was noisy, but uneventful. The group was met by the **exemplary** guide they had requested. She told them that they would be taking the space tram to begin their tour of the capital.

The tour guide explained that the word capital was **derived** from the Latin root *caput* meaning head. "We head up the capitalization process for the galaxy. As you know, capitalization is very important. Without it, we could not tell the difference between nouns and names. For example, let's say your dog's name is Spike."

A couple of the kids could be heard exclaiming that their dog's name was Spike. "Okay, great. You have a dog named Spike. Without capitalization and some punctuation, you wouldn't know if the sentence, *I ordered spike the ball*, meant that you were to throw the football at the ground or if I was telling my dog Spike to get the ball." The students nodded that they understood.

We capitalize all proper nouns here. "Can anyone tell me what a proper noun is?" the guide asked.

She called upon an eager girl who was raising her hand as vigorously as she could. "A proper noun is one with a specific name. Girl is a common noun but my name, Heather, is a proper noun. It should be capitalized." She looked around her after she finished speaking to make sure everyone had seen her give the correct answer.

"Show off!" Luke whispered. Kirk heard him and glared at him. Luke shrugged apologetically.

"That's right, Heather!" the guide said. "There have been so many famous names that were capitalized right here. You're going to learn more about them on your trip today. But what's really exciting is that every one of you had your name capitalized here too – even if you're not famous!"

The children giggled and chattered with one another about being big names in the galaxy. The tour guide continued. "There are men and women who live here full-time and make sure that all proper nouns are capitalized. You'll get to meet some of them today and ask them questions about their work. Who knows? Maybe some of you will want to work in the capital someday," she said, smiling at a few faces.

The children began discussing the possibility of working in the capital. The tour guide quieted them to point out the import/export area of the city. "This is where words up for capitalization come into the city. It's also where newly capitalized words are sent from the city."

The children pressed their faces against the windows of the tram to see the lines of words. "Wow! Cool!" they said as they watched the lines of words moving quickly. "It's so fast!" the tour guide heard them saying.

"It is indeed a speedy process. We have to move millions of words through the city. We can't afford slow lines or it would cause problems on planet English." The children nodded.

The tram soon stopped at a park, where the children and their chaperones ate the picnic lunches they'd brought with them. After half an hour, the tour guide used a bullhorn to announce that they would be leaving for the Capitol building in five minutes. Many of the children cheered.

Once inside the Capitol building, the guide and the group walked down the Hall of Names. The children were impressed by the important names of history whose paintings hung there. They were most excited about modern people whose paintings they spotted. As they continued to walk, the tour guide pointed out paintings of famous buildings and products as well. Some of the children wanted their picture taken with a particular painting. The tour guide reminded them that no flash could be used in order to protect the paintings.

"The next stop on our tour is the original *Capitalization Constitution*. We keep it under glass to protect it. It's very old, but we still use it here in the Capitol to make capitalization decisions." She led the group to a round room with a glass case in the center. "Gather around, but make sure you allow everyone a chance to see it close up," she said.

The little girl, who had been first to say what a proper noun was, arrived first at the case. "It isn't here!" she declared.

"Of course it's there," the guide said, walking close to the case. As their guide reached the case, she turned pale and began looking wildly about. "Where is it?"

The three English children noticed the guide's panic. Kirk approached her. "What's wrong?"

"The *Capitalization Constitution* is missing," she said, shaking.

"Could it be on display somewhere temporarily? Perhaps they forgot to inform you," Kirk said.

"No. It's never moved. We have to have it to capitalize words," she said, her voice growing more high pitched as she spoke.

"We'll help. Don't worry," Kirk promised her.

Kirk contacted his father via communicator. When the king answered, he was on the golf course and very surprised to hear from Kirk. "What's wrong?" he asked with concern.

"The *Capitalization Constitution* is missing!" Kirk told him.

The king's face registered alarm. "You're kidding. And right when I was shooting the best game of my life. I imagine the Gremlin is behind this. I'll contact the GBI for help in locating it."

"Our guide says the capitalization process will come to a standstill until we find it," Kirk said. The tour guide heard Kirk and seemed panicky. "Is there anything we can do?" Kirk added.

"Yes, Kirk, there is. Use the space porter to come back. Read the entry on tricky capitalization in *The Guidebook to Grammar Galaxy*. Then send out a mission to the guardians. They can help the Capitol with the process until the Constitution can be recovered."

"Thanks, Father. Good luck with the rest of your game."

The king sighed and disconnected, doubting whether he could recover after the upsetting phone call. And he still had to contact the GBI.

Kirk told the tour guide his plan and he and his family left immediately for the castle. In the castle library, he read the entry on tricky capitalization to his mother and siblings.

Tricky Capitalization

Names of people, pets, places, and things are capitalized. But some capitalization rules for proper nouns can be tricky.

People and pets. People's titles are capitalized when used as a name. President Lincoln is capitalized. But in the sentence *Lincoln was the 16th president.*, the word *president* is not capitalized. Nicknames are capitalized, such as Air Jordan. Languages and nationalities are capitalized. For example, French and East Indian. The words black and white referring to race aren't capitalized. Religions and religious terms are capitalized, such as Hindu or Buddhist. Bible is capitalized but biblical is not. Organizations like the Red Cross and Green Bay Packers are capitalized as are government entities like Congress. The part of dog or cat breeds that is derived from a proper noun is capitalized and the rest is not. For example, Yorkshire terrier.

Places. Buildings with a specific name are capitalized as in the Empire State Building. The word *the* is not capitalized unless it is a required part of the name as in The Louvre Museum. Astronomical names like Neptune and Pluto are capitalized, while sun and moon generally aren't. Regions are capitalized, while directions are not. For example, *I am heading west to live in Southern California*. Streets or road names are capitalized. Cities, counties, and countries are capitalized. The words city and county are only capitalized as part of the name. For example, *I have never been to the city of New York, but I think New York City would be a great place to visit*.

Things. Days and months are capitalized, but seasons are not. For example, *I see that Friday is the first day of spring.* Events, holidays, and eras are capitalized, such as the Great Depression, the Olympic Games, and the Renaissance.
Specific course names like Economics 101 are capitalized while the subject matter of economics is not. Only the proper name part of a disease is capitalized, such as Alzheimer's disease. Only a specific type of plant or recipe name is capitalized. For example, Japanese maple or Grammar Galaxy grapefruit. Trademarks like Coca Cola are capitalized.

When confused about capitalization, an Internet search can help.

"No wonder they need a Constitution to figure this out!" Luke exclaimed.

"For now, the guidebook is going to be the Constitution and the guardians are going to be serving the Capitol," Kirk said. "Let's get this mission on tricky capitalization out right away."

What does *derived* mean?

Why couldn't the Capitol decide which words to capitalize?

Why does it matter if words are capitalized?

Unit III: Adventures in Grammar

Chapter 15

"What have you been studying lately?" the king asked at dinner one evening.

Luke was the first to respond. "We've been learning about American history."

"Yes, it's interesting. But what I don't understand is why they would want to dump perfectly good tea into the harbor," Ellen said.

"It isn't that they didn't like tea. They were protesting the taxes they had to pay," the king said.

"But everyone has to pay taxes, don't they, Father?" Kirk asked.

"It has to do with representational government, Kirk. The people of America wanted to have a say in their laws. They didn't want a tax they hadn't voted for. They wanted to be free above all else."

"Right!" Luke exclaimed. "That's why Patrick Henry said, 'Give me, give me.' Ugh, I know it. He said, 'Give me—.' Why can't I remember?" Look smacked his forehead with his palm.

"Oh, you mean 'Give me—, give me—.' That's strange. I can't think of it either," Kirk said.

"That's a quote worth remembering," the king said. "Why don't you two look it up and tell me what it is later." Kirk looked at the screen and was about to ask for help when the king corrected him. "Find it yourself and then you're more likely to remember it," he **lectured**.

★ ★ ★ ★ ★ ★ ★ ★ ★ ★

lectured – *taught*

★ ★ ★ ★ ★ ★ ★ ★ ★ ★

"Okay, we'll look it up after dinner," Kirk promised.

"I like their Declaration of—, of something. They said they had, you know, I can't think of the word. But I remember it was good. Okay, I have something else to look up after dinner," Luke said, laughing.

The rest of the family laughed too.

After dinner, the three English children used their history books to find the information they couldn't recall. "Here it is!" Kirk exclaimed. "Patrick Henry was opposed to the Stamp Act. That act required the American colonists to produce all printed materials using paper that was taxed. Patrick Henry said there should be no...that's odd. There are words missing here." Kirk picked up the book to examine it closely. He wondered if it was a printing problem, but the rest of the ink looked okay. He looked at the paragraph again. "He is famous for saying, 'Give me...this word is missing too! We need to tell Father."

The three children found their father in his study. He noted that they had a history book with them. "Oh good, you reviewed your lessons. Do you remember what Patrick Henry said now?"

"No, it isn't in here," Kirk said, handing him the book.

"You're kidding. Who wrote this book? Is he rewriting...rewriting, hm. I can't say the word. Did he leave out the...the.... Oh, for grammar's sake. What's wrong with it?" the king stammered.

"There are words missing," Kirk explained, pointing to the blank spaces in the paragraph he had been reading.

"It hasn't been whited out. And the print seems to be okay. There's only one explanation for this," the king began.

"The Gremlin," the kids said in a chorus.

"What has he done this time?" Kirk asked.

"There is a particular type of word missing here," the king said.

"Is it a noun, verb, adjective, adverb, or preposition?" Luke asked, proud of his knowledge of parts of speech.

"Nouns appear to be missing, Luke. But not all nouns. Patrick Henry is a proper noun and that is listed here. I see the Stamp Act and paper, too. I think I know what's missing, but I don't know why."

"Tell us!" Ellen urged her father.

"All right. Let's head to the library and get *The Guidebook to Grammar Galaxy.* I want to read you an article on a particular type of noun that we haven't discussed before," the king said.

Once in the royal library, the king read the entry on abstract nouns.

Abstract Nouns

Abstract nouns are concepts, ideas, experiences, traits, qualities, feelings, and states of being that cannot be experienced with the five senses. **Concrete nouns** are the opposite of abstract nouns and can be seen, heard, smelled, tasted, or touched.

If you aren't sure whether an abstract noun is a noun, replace it with a concrete noun in a sentence. If it makes sense, it's a noun. For example, <u>I lost my joy.</u> Replace the word *joy* with the concrete noun, *necklace*. Because <u>I lost my necklace.</u> makes sense, *joy* is a noun.

The following are examples of abstract nouns.
Emotions/Feelings
Love
Sadness
Happiness
Anger
Peace
Character Traits/States of Being
Beauty
Integrity
Honesty
Bravery
Skill

Concepts/Ideas
Liberty
Faith
Dream
Belief
Truth
Events/Experiences
Friendship
Culture
Education
Progress
Leisure

Some nouns may be difficult to classify as abstract or concrete, like *death*. *Child* is a concrete noun, but *childhood* is abstract. Writers should use concrete nouns to explain abstract nouns in their writing to make their meaning clear.

"You're right, Father! Abstract nouns were definitely missing from our history book," Kirk said. "But what has the Gremlin done this time to cause the problem?"

"That's what we need to find out," the king said. "Screen, can you tell me anything about abstract nouns on planet Sentence?" he asked.

"Your Majesty, abstract nouns are being sent to planet Recycling," Screen replied.

"What? Why? This is outrageous!" the king roared.

"It seems that the new Observation Act is being applied to them," Screen explained.

"Great grammar, I hadn't thought of that. The Gremlin has obviously **exploited** this ct for his own purposes," the king said.

"What's the Observation Act?" Luke asked.

"Parliament passed a law, stating that we will only print facts – what we can see, hear, taste, smell, or touch. I'm going to have to call an emergency session of Parliament to **repeal** the act. But this is an emergency for you too. Send out a mission to the guardians. When they identify abstract

★ ★ ★ ★ ★ ★ ★ ★ ★ ★

exploited – *misused*

repeal – *cancel*

★ ★ ★ ★ ★ ★ ★ ★ ★ ★

nouns, you can travel to planet Sentence and rescue them from being recycled. Imagine our galaxy without abstract nouns!" the king said.

The children responded to their father's urgent request and sent out a mission called "Abstract Nouns" immediately.

What does *exploited* mean?

Why were some words missing from the history book?

What is the difference between an abstract and a concrete noun?

Chapter 16

The English children were excited to be in a special class with their peers. Their local police chief would be talking to them about safety.

Luke was most excited about seeing Max, the police dog, in action. The police chief indulged him by having the German shepherd demonstrate his searching behavior. The police chief told the children, "Some police dogs are trained using German commands, mostly by tradition. Our dogs won't listen to a criminal's commands, so we can use English to train them too. Max is our K9 partner. He watches our behavior and listens to our commands. If I look nervous and back up from someone, Max will begin barking and baring his teeth. Max, brummen," he said. The dog growled at the door. "Good boy!" he said. The children clapped their approval.

"We wanted to introduce you to Max because he's our most popular officer. But we also wanted to talk with you about how to stay safe. There are lots of ways to protect yourself. Who here wears a helmet when riding a bike?" Many hands shot up. "That's good! Very few bicyclists with serious injuries were wearing helmets. It's a simple thing we can all do to stay safe.

"We also want to talk with you about a new way for you to stay safe. To make sure that you are being picked up by an approved adult or to identify you if you're missing, we are asking you to use our Appositive app. We will scan your fingerprint and your eye. We will add a picture of you and information like your height, weight, and blood type. The app will tell us who is allowed to give you rides or make decisions for you. We like to say the app helps us be positive about who you are. We have officers standing by to help you add your information to the app. Your parents will have to approve everything before your account will become active. Before we break up to do that, I want to share some tips with you.

"First, do not go with anyone your parent hasn't given you permission to go with. For example, if your friend's parent offers to give you a ride home from spaceball practice, be sure to get your parent's permission first. Second, if you need help, ask someone who is in charge first. Seek a police officer or someone who works at the place where you are. Third, if you feel uncomfortable with someone other than your parent, it is okay to say no or run away. It may be a misunderstanding, but it's better to be rude and stay safe. Finally, refuse to keep secrets, unless it's about a gift or surprise. If anyone threatens you for revealing a secret, ask for help."

The group of children listened attentively and **soberly**. "Are there any questions?" the police chief asked.

★ ★ ★ ★ ★ ★ ★ ★ ★ ★

soberly – *seriously*

★ ★ ★ ★ ★ ★ ★ ★ ★ ★

A young girl raised her hand and said, "My sister always wants me to keep it secret that she has been eating candy." The group laughed. The chief said, "Her secret is out now." He directed the children to line up to start using the Appositive app.

The queen spoke to the chief while the children waited in line. "This was a wonderful presentation and a good reminder. Thank you for doing this."

"My pleasure, Your Highness," he said.

"The Appositive app is such a brilliant idea too."

"We are hopeful that it will help us keep kids safe," he agreed.

At dinner that evening, Kirk, Luke, Ellen, and the queen filled their father in on the safety presentation.

"The police chief, an impressive man, was a good speaker," Kirk said.

"He taught us some rules, principles of safety, we can use," Ellen added.

"We got to meet Max, their K9 officer, too," Luke said.

"The children got to add their information to an app, the Appositive app, to keep them safe," the queen said.

"The Appositive app, a safety app, is a good idea," the king said. The queen explained how it worked.

"So all of that information is stored in the Appositive app, a safety app? Why did I say that again like that? The Appositive app, a safety app? Do you all know what an appositive is?" The three children shook their heads no. The king requested *The Guidebook to Grammar Galaxy*. When it was brought to him, he said, "This book, *The*

Guidebook to Grammar Galaxy, will explain what an appositive is. Great grammar! I've done it again. I better just read."

Appositives

An appositive is a noun or noun phrase that is used to give more information about another noun. Nonessential appositives are set off with commas. For example, Scientists monitor potentially hazardous asteroids, space rocks larger than 100 meters. Appositives can appear at the beginning, middle, or end of a sentence.

Essential appositives are required for the sentence to be meaningful. Essential appositives are not set off with commas. For example, Ben's friend Milo is coming over today. In this sentence, *Milo* is essential information. Otherwise, we would not know which friend was coming over.

"The guidebook, our essential language arts reference, explained that very well," Kirk said. "Wait! I just used a nonessential appositive, didn't I? I didn't mean to," he added.

"Yes. This is why I'm concerned," the king said. "Screen," he commanded, "please give me a status report on planet Sentence."

Screen began playing a video. A reporter said, "I'm here in Noun Town where there is mass confusion. The king's new safety **edict,** requiring positive identification of all nouns appears to be the cause. Appositives have **proliferated** and there is crowding here in Noun Town."

★ ★ ★ ★ ★ ★ ★ ★ ★ ★
edict – *law*
proliferated – *multiplied*
★ ★ ★ ★ ★ ★ ★ ★ ★ ★

When the video ended, the king added, "And the end result is we are overusing appositives here on planet English. I am going to do what I can to clean up this mess, the overcrowding because of an edict I didn't create. I need you children to send out a mission. Have the guardians identify appositives. Then you'll need to go to Noun Town and oversee their removal."

The three English children agreed and got to work on a mission called "Appositives."

What is an *edict*?

What is an appositive?

Why was the royal family overusing appositives?

Chapter 17

"I'm so excited to go over and see the Tumult triplets," Ellen gushed.

"I know," the queen agreed. "The pictures Mrs. Tumult sent are absolutely precious. But I can't imagine having three babies at once! Life was hard enough when I had you children one at a time."

Ellen laughed. "Do you think Mrs. Tumult will let me hold them?" she asked.

"I have a feeling she will be happy to let anyone hold them," the queen said, smiling.

Once at the Tumult residence, Ellen was **transfixed**. The babies were so cute. She couldn't stop looking at them. The queen asked Mrs. Tumult about the delivery and their weights. The new mother looked exhausted, the queen couldn't help but notice. "Do you have enough help?" she asked her friend.

★ ★ ★ ★ ★ ★ ★ ★ ★ ★

transfixed – *fascinated*

★ ★ ★ ★ ★ ★ ★ ★ ★ ★

"I had a lot of help when I first brought them home, but now not as much. My husband is working, and my mother had to go back home." Mrs. Tumult looked so sad.

The queen was about to offer words of encouragement when Ellen interjected. "I could come over and help! I would love to hold them. I could feed them too if you show me how. You could rest while I helped."

The queen and Mrs. Tumult looked at one another and smiled. They knew she didn't know how hard it could be to take care of three babies at once. Even so, the queen was proud of her daughter for offering.

"Ellen, that's so nice of you, but..." Mrs. Tumult began.

"I'm not offering to be nice. I *want* to help!" Ellen insisted.

"Well..." Mrs. Tumult said hesitantly, looking to her friend. "Are you all right with Ellen spending a few hours a week here to help me?"

"Absolutely!" the queen said. "As you can see, Ellen loves babies. And maybe it would give you a break. I know you could use some sleep."

Mrs. Tumult smiled gratefully. "That I could."

"When can I start?" Ellen asked eagerly.

"I think my husband would be agreeable to Ellen using the space porter for this purpose. She could come by herself then," the queen offered.

"How about tomorrow? Do you have time?" Mrs. Tumult asked.

"May I, Mother?" Ellen asked pleadingly.

"I don't see why not. But your studies have to be finished," the queen said.

"I'll work quickly so I can come over in the afternoon. Is that okay?" Ellen asked. Mrs. Tumult agreed, and a time was set for the following day.

Ellen breezed through her homework and turned Cook down on the snack she offered her. She wanted to get to the Tumult residence as quickly as possible.

Mrs. Tumult seemed relieved to see her. "I have to warn you. They've been very fussy today," she said.

"That's okay. I don't mind," Ellen reassured her. She smiled at the babies. "You're Alyssa, you're Ben, and you're Caleb. I know what it's like to have two brothers, Alyssa. I'll help you," she said, rubbing Alyssa's belly. Alyssa responded by getting quiet and staring at Ellen. "See, Mrs. Tumult? I've got this," she said confidently.

"Okay," Mrs. Tumult said, somewhat less confidently. "The babies have been fed and their diapers have been changed. I'll teach you how to change them next time you come. But honestly, I just need a nap. Are you okay if I go lie down? I'll be just down the hall if you need me," she said.

"Of course!" Ellen assured her. "We'll be just fine, won't we?" she said, cooing at the babies.

"Thank you so much, Ellen," Mrs. Tumult said wearily.

Ellen was sure she could keep the babies quiet and happy, so Mrs. Tumult could sleep.

Alyssa was looking intently at Ellen, so Ellen spoke to her in a sing-song voice. Ben started to fuss, so Ellen started to comfort him. He calmed down. Then Alyssa let out a wail. As she tried to console Alyssa, Caleb started to cry.

Ellen had an idea. She would try to hold all three babies at once. Then none of them would cry. Once she had them in position, she sang to them. That seemed to work for a few minutes. Then she recited nursery rhymes. When that quit working, she tried gently bouncing them. Each of her babysitting tricks worked for less and less time. Soon she felt like joining the babies in crying. *How does Mrs. Tumult do it?* Ellen wondered.

Time moved at a glacial pace until the babies' mother emerged from her room. When Mrs. Tumult saw and heard the crying, she hurried to help. "No luck soothing them, huh?" she asked.

"No. I'm so sorry! It all started crying at once. Alyssa didn't want his rattle. Ben and Caleb wanted hers for a while. It seems like I would get one of them quiet and then it would start crying again."

Mrs. Tumult looked quizzically at Ellen. "I'm afraid this was all too much for you, Ellen. I'm sorry to put you through it."

"Oh no! I enjoyed taking care of the babies and playing with him," Ellen reassured her.

"Which him? Ben or Caleb?" Mrs. Tumult asked.

"Oh, she was both great. Alyssa is great too and I liked holding him. I just wanted the babies to have her playtime, so you could rest. I feel bad that I couldn't keep it happy."

Mrs. Tumult was concerned. She patted Ellen on the shoulder. "Taking care of three babies at once is a challenge for anyone. I know you did your best."

Later that evening, Mrs. Tumult called the queen. "Ellen is a lovely girl," she began. "You should be so proud of her."

"Oh, thank you," the queen replied gratefully. "Did she allow you to get some rest?"

"Yes. Unfortunately, the babies didn't cooperate though. They have been so fussy lately. I wanted to call to thank you for sending Ellen. But I also wanted to tell you I am a little worried."

"Oh?" the queen asked, a little worried herself.

"When I got up from my nap, Ellen seemed pretty frazzled. That's understandable. What was a concern was how she kept referring to Alyssa as him, the boys as her, and all the babies as it. I'm just hoping I haven't given her too much responsibility."

"Oh, don't worry. I'm sure she's fine. She was probably just afraid you would be disappointed in her," the queen said reassuringly.

"Oh no. That wasn't it at all. I couldn't make these babies happy. I certainly didn't expect your daughter to."

The two women continued chatting. The queen encouraged her friend that one day she would be able to sleep again. Mrs. Tumult felt much better.

When the queen ended the call, she sought out Ellen to see what she thought of babysitting.

"I spoke to Mrs. Tumult," the queen began when she found Ellen.

"You did?" Ellen asked. "Was she mad? I couldn't get the babies to stop his crying. I tried really hard to comfort it, Mother. But I guess I'm just not cut out for babysitting," she said, sighing.

"Nonsense, Ellen. Those babies had been fussing all day. Even their mother couldn't get them settled. But I'm worried that the stress is too much for you. You called the babies 'it.' Do you need a nap? I wouldn't blame you," the queen said.

"Did he say I was calling the babies the wrong names? I thought I got all her names right. I was careful about that," Ellen said, feeling defensive.

"He who? Do you mean your father?" the queen asked.

"No, Mrs. Tumult. Did they say he was unhappy with my babysitting?" Ellen asked, getting more agitated by the moment.

"Now you're talking about they and I don't know what you mean." The queen stopped herself and hugged her daughter. "You've been so excited about babysitting. You didn't sleep well last night, did you?" Ellen shook her head no and her eyes filled with tears. "All right. I insist you take a nap. You'll feel better. I promise. I'm so proud of you, Ellen. Mrs. Tumult said you were a lovely girl and you are."

Ellen went to her bedchamber dutifully. She had to admit she was exhausted. The queen went to tell her husband what Mrs. Tumult had said. She was a little worried about Ellen and wanted confirmation that this was just fatigue.

The queen found the king in the gym. Normally, the queen wouldn't interrupt his workout, but he seemed to be finishing.

"What's going on, my dear?" he asked cheerfully.

"Ellen got home from babysitting for Mrs. Tumult," she replied.

"Ah, yes. How did it go?" the king asked, wiping the sweat from his brow.

"The babies were fussy today and he wouldn't settle no matter what Ellen did," she explained.

"So just one of the boys wouldn't settle?" the king asked.

"Unfortunately, none of the babies settled and so they were really stressed about it."

"Mrs. Tumult and Ellen were stressed?" the king asked.

"Mostly just Ellen. In fact, Mrs. Tumult called and told me that Ellen was so stressed she was calling all the babies 'it.' They were worried that it was too much for Ellen."

"So, Mr. Tumult was also concerned?" the king asked, getting confused.

"I don't think so. She didn't mention talking to her," the queen said.

"You mean she didn't talk to Ellen about her concerns?" the king asked, getting a bit agitated.

"She didn't talk to Ellen, but I meant that she hadn't talked to her, Mr. Tumult," the queen said, clearly annoyed. "I can see that you are preoccupied. We can talk about this after you've had a shower." The queen left the gym and the king thought about the **perplexing** conversation he had just had with his wife.

★ ★ ★ ★ ★ ★ ★ ★ ★

perplexing – *confusing*

★ ★ ★ ★ ★ ★ ★ ★ ★

Mrs. Tumult, I think, said that Ellen was confusing her pronouns. She thought it was due to stress from watching the babies. In telling me what happened, the queen was confusing pronouns too. This can't be stress. Something is wrong on planet Sentence, he thought.

He decided to do some research to be sure. "Screen, you need us to give it a status report on planet Sentence, please," he said, once in his study.

Screen hesitated before responding with "Certainly, Your Majesty. I am not seeing anything in the news."

"That honestly doesn't surprise it. This would most likely be a private disagreement. He needs to find the kids and talk to them about her," the king said.

"Are you tired, Your Majesty?" Screen asked.

"A little, like I always am after my workouts," the king answered. Why does she ask?"

"Your speech isn't what I expect," Screen explained **tactfully**.

★ ★ ★ ★ ★ ★ ★ ★ ★

tactfully – *considerately*

★ ★ ★ ★ ★ ★ ★ ★ ★

"The problem is spreading. You will talk to the kids," the king said.

"Sire?" Screen asked.

"I mean I will!" he said, getting frustrated.

He found Kirk and Luke and decided to let Ellen rest. He asked them to accompany him to the library. There he read them an entry on pronoun-antecedent agreement.

Pronoun-Antecedent Agreement
A **pronoun** takes the place of a noun so sentences aren't repetitive. A noun that comes before and is replaced by a pronoun is called an **antecedent**. *Ante* means

before. For example, <u>The captain encouraged his crew.</u> The possessive pronoun *his* refers to the antecedent *captain*. Pronouns and antecedents must agree or match in number and gender.

<u>Singular or Plural Agreement</u>. A singular pronoun must have a singular antecedent. The pronouns *I, me, my, he, him, his, she, her, hers, it,* and *its* are singular. The nouns these pronouns replace must also be singular or one in number.

The pronouns *we, our, ours, they, them, their,* and *theirs* are plural and should replace plural nouns or those that number more than one.

A prepositional phrase or clause after the noun does not determine the number of the pronoun. For example, <u>The box of lasers was placed on its shelf.</u> *Lasers* in the prepositional phrase is plural, but *box* is singular, requiring the singular pronoun *its*.

Compound subjects joined by *and* always take a plural pronoun. For example, <u>All moons and our moon orbit their planets.</u> Even though *moon* is singular, the plural possessive pronoun *their* is used because it is a compound subject.

Compound subjects joined by *or/nor* use a singular or plural pronoun depending on whether the noun closest to the pronoun is singular or plural. For example, <u>Our planet or other planets follow their orbit around the sun.</u> *Planets* is closest, so the plural possessive pronoun *their* is used. <u>Neither the dogs nor cat will eat its lunch.</u> *Cat* is closest, so the singular possessive pronoun *its* is used.

Titles or single subjects take a singular pronoun. <u>*Number the Stars* has its fans.</u> <u>Mumps is making its way through college campuses.</u>

<u>Gender Agreement</u>. Male nouns should use *he, him,* or *his*. Female nouns should use *she, her,* or *hers*. Gender neutral nouns should use *it, its, or plural pronouns*.

When human gender is either or unknown, writers may use both male and female pronouns with the conjunction *or*. <u>A student should have his or her book for class.</u> Using a plural noun makes for a simpler sentence, however. <u>Students should have their books for class.</u>

Using *they* or *their* with a singular, unknown gender antecedent has also become acceptable in modern usage. <u>Your sibling may want to have their own room.</u>

"She has a problem," Luke said.

"Who has a problem?" the king asked.

"She does," Luke said, gesturing to the three of them.

The king sighed. "I know what you mean, but you can't say it. I need you two to go to planet Sentence and get the pronouns and antecedents back into agreement. I have a feeling the Gremlin has been up to her old tricks again." The king grimaced as he realized he used the wrong pronoun. "And one more thing. We need the guardians' help to get it back in agreement as soon as possible."

The two boys nodded, understanding what their father meant to say. They created a mission called "Pronoun-Antecedent Agreement." Then they left for planet Sentence using the space porter.

What does *tactfully* mean?

What are some examples of singular pronouns?

Who did the king suspect were having a disagreement on planet Sentence?

Chapter 18

Luke had been looking forward to that night's spaceball game all season. His team, the Astros, would be playing their rivals, the Cosmos. They had never beaten them, but Luke had a good feeling about the game.

The royal family would be in attendance, something the reporters had gotten used to. The focus would rightfully remain on the game.

Luke had recently been playing catcher and he enjoyed the position. He always had something to do when they were playing defense. He told himself that his mission for the night was not to let a ball get past him.

At the ballpark, Luke could feel the nervous energy amongst his teammates. He began warming up with their starting pitcher. Luke could see the determination in his eyes. "You've got...you've got..." Luke called to him. *That's weird*, Luke thought. I must be nervous. *Shake it off*, he told himself.

"Batter up!" the umpire called after they'd practiced for a while. Luke took a deep breath from behind home plate and gave the pitcher the sign for a fastball. That was his best pitch. Luke was delighted when the ball was heading right for his glove. He prepared himself for the smack that meant a strike when he heard the crack of a bat instead. The ball sailed into center field. The batter took off and soon rounded first base.

"Catch!" the royal family members were yelling from the stands. The center fielder positioned himself under the ball and extended his glove. The ball hit the glove. The crowd was elated and then disappointed when the ball bounced off to the ground.

"Throw! Throw!" the crowd began yelling. The center fielder recovered. He threw the ball to the infield, but not before the batter had reached third base. Luke pounded his catcher's mitt in frustration. *This isn't a good start*, he thought.

He could see the alarm on the pitcher's face. "You've got...we're good," Luke said to reassure him. He was happy to see the boy relax.

Luke signaled for an inside change-up pitch for the next batter. The pitcher nodded. Once again, Luke waited for the impact of the ball in his glove and heard a thwack as the bat connected instead. The first baseman ran to the grounder, picked it up, and ran to tag first base for the out. "Throw!" the crowd called. It took a moment for the player to recall the play. Then he threw the ball to Luke with all the power he could **muster**.

★ ★ ★ ★ ★ ★ ★ ★ ★ ★

muster – *create*

euphoric – *overjoyed*

exchange– *conversation*

★ ★ ★ ★ ★ ★ ★ ★ ★ ★

Luke refused to look at the runner coming from third and concentrated on catching the ball. The moment it hit his mitt, Luke swept his arm across the left side of the plate. He connected with the runner a split second before his foot touched it. Dust billowed around them and there was silence before the umpire called, "Out!"

The fans of the Astros were **euphoric**. The royal family high-fived one another. But the Cosmos's coach was furious. He marched out to the umpire and had a heated **exchange** because he didn't think his player was out. The umpire refused to change his call. Luke was shocked when the coach began kicking dirt at the umpire.

The king was irritated by this behavior and called, "Throw!" As soon as he did so, he was confused. "Throw?" he said questioningly.

"Eject!" Kirk cried.

"Yes, eject!" the king agreed, though he thought to himself that they were speaking strangely.

The umpire signaled that the coach was thrown out for the rest of the game. The assistant coach took over, but the Cosmos's fans were agitated.

When the Astros first batter was up, he was struck by a wild pitch. "Take..." Kirk started to call to him. He couldn't say what he meant to say and told his father. "I think something is wrong."

"I know! The Cosmos are poor sports," the king said angrily.

"No, Father, I mean I'm not talking right."

"Well, that's what happens when people don't play by the rules," the king said. "I'm so mad I'm not talking right either."

"What I mean is I am missing some words," Kirk explained.

"I have some words I'm not saying too because I'd be in trouble with your mother," the king joked.

Kirk sighed. "Father, I mean I am not able to finish some of my sentences. Like I can't say anything after throw or catch. Can you?"

"Throw...catch...great grammar, you're right, Kirk."

"What could be causing...?" Kirk asked.

"I'm going to eat a..." the king said. Kirk wondered why his father was thinking about eating when there was a serious problem in the galaxy. Then he continued. "Just as I thought. Direct objects seem to be missing, Kirk. Would you and Ellen be willing to handle...can you help? Your mother and I can watch...and I can eat."

Kirk and Ellen agreed to return to the castle using the space porter. There they could research the problem. They promised to report back using the communicator as soon as possible.

"Not really," Ellen admitted.

"We need to look them up in the guidebook." The two ran to the library and opened the guidebook to an entry on transitive and intransitive verbs.

Direct Objects

A direct object is a noun receiving the action of a transitive verb.

In the sentence, <u>The girl ate ice cream.</u>, *ate* is an action verb and *ice cream* is the direct object. To find the direct object, ask *what* after the action verb. The girl ate what? Ice cream.

There are no direct objects with intransitive verbs. Some verbs are always intransitive like *go*, *sit*, *lie*, and *die*. Others may be either transitive or intransitive. In the sentence <u>The girl eats.</u>, *eats* is intransitive. There is no direct object.

"I remember...Transitive verbs are verbs with wheels that transport action to another word. It's a problem that the direct objects are missing."

"If I can't eat... like the girl, I agree," Ellen said.

The two asked Screen to tell them anything unusual happening on planet Sentence. In just a few moments, Screen produced a news story on protests taking place on the planet. People carried signs that read, "No action without permission" and "Objects have rights too." Transitive verbs were being run out of verb village by the angry mob. Many nouns were in the crowd, wearing banners that read, "Former direct object."

"I never thought about how hard life would be as a direct object. All those transitive verbs doing...to you without permission," Ellen said.

"Ellen, the English language is shutting down! This isn't a real problem. This is the Gremlin's doing, I'm sure," Kirk said.

"But what about their rights?" Ellen asked.

"Ellen, they're not being abused!" Kirk said, getting frustrated. "This is what words do. Wait, let's tell Father and he'll agree with me." Kirk called the king on his communicator and explained the protests. He also mentioned that Ellen was sympathetic to the direct objects.

"Ellen, I promise you that direct objects do not suffer. But the whole galaxy will suffer if you guardians don't put a stop to this," the king explained.

The king said he would contact his event planner immediately. A rally would be held on planet Sentence to honor direct objects and their transitive verbs. Kirk and Ellen would ask the guardians to identify the words that should be invited in a mission called "Direct Objects." The king was hopeful that the rally would break up the protests and solve the galaxy's language problem.

What does *euphoric* mean?

What did the king want to watch while Kirk and Ellen returned to the castle?

What is a direct object?

Chapter 19

The king was more excited than Luke was about the spaceball game that evening. He remembered getting the call from the galaxy's most popular spaceball sportscaster. He had invited Luke to be a guest announcer. The king had been **jubilant** when he told Luke. Luke appeared pleased at first, but he grew more anxious as the game grew closer.

★ ★ ★ ★ ★ ★ ★ ★ ★ ★

jubilant – *thrilled*

★ ★ ★ ★ ★ ★ ★ ★ ★ ★

The king understood. Luke would be on galactic television, announcing a major league game. That was a lot of pressure for a young man. The king knew just the thing to put Luke at ease: he would have him practice announcing the game.

Every televised game leading up to Luke's night in the booth, the king had Luke pretending to be the announcer. "What would you say here, Luke?" he would prod him.

"Uhh," Luke would often respond.

"Luke, just pretend you're talking with me. You don't have to have anything **profound** to say," the king **exhorted** him.

profound – *great*

exhorted – *urged*

After a few weeks of this, the king felt Luke was ready. Luke was fairly confident too. *It isn't that hard*, he thought. He repeated those words to reassure himself as his father led him into the stadium. Luke could tell his father was nervous too.

"I can't wait to meet these guys," the king said.

"You haven't met the sportscasters before?" Luke asked.

"No. I've met many major league players but never the guys in the booth," the king said.

"Don't be scared," Luke joked.

The king laughed and it did decrease his anxiety.

A security guard let the two of them in a secured door where the game was broadcast on television. Luke and the king shook the two sportscasters' hands. The king made some small talk. Eventually, the announcers and the sound engineer made it clear that the king needed to leave. Luke could tell he was disappointed. "Are you going to watch me, Father?" Luke asked.

"Of course! I am going to watch one of the screens inside the stadium," he said, patting Luke on the shoulder. "You'll do great. Most of all, I want you to have fun."

"Thanks, Father. I will," Luke said.

"Thanks so much for bringing him up, Your Majesty," one of the announcers said. "You have a fine boy here."

When the king left, Luke was told where to sit and where to look. The sound engineer had him speak into the microphone for a sound check. He gave Luke a thumb's up. "Great volume!" he told Luke. Luke found himself relaxing a bit.

He chatted more with the two announcers until it was game time. That's when he started to get nervous again. A red light on the camera indicated that they were live. The more famous sportscaster said, "It's a beautiful night for a ballgame, folks! I think we are in for a treat with these two teams. But we also have a special guest with us this evening—Luke English, the king and queen's youngest son. Luke, welcome!"

"Thank you. I'm honored to be here," Luke started. Inside, Luke was relieved he had gotten past his first statement.

"Luke, I understand you've been playing catcher for your team, the Astros. How do you like that position?"

"I like it a lot. I'm always a part of the action. I just wish my batting average were better."

All three men in the booth laughed. "You're in good company with that wish, Luke," one of them told him.

The king was watching the broadcast on a screen near a snack stand. He was ecstatic with how Luke was doing. He ignored the people who were gawking at him when they realized who he was.

Back in the booth, the second announcer was talking about the fielding team, the Meteors. "What do you think of their season, Luke?"

"The Meteors is a great ball club. Their starting pitcher play with a lot of passion," Luke said confidently.

The announcer seemed surprised by what Luke said, so Luke tried to justify it. "The Planets is a good club too. But I likes the Meteors' chances better tonight."

The announcer in the booth and the king watching near the snack stand had the same reaction. Why is he talking like that? Both men chalked it up to nerves and hoped the next time Luke spoke that everything would be fine.

The two announcers chatted with one another about the gameplay for an inning before talking with Luke again. One announcer asked him what he thought. "The Meteors' pitcher don't let nerves get to him. This team run practices focused on the mental game," Luke said. He was particularly proud that he had studied the Meteors' approach off the field.

Again with the weird speech, the sportscasters thought.

"There are a question I have for you now," Luke continued boldly. "Are Elliot or Martinez the better shortstop?"

The sportscaster to Luke's right stuttered. *Ha! I'm more prepared than they are*, Luke thought.

"It's hard to say, isn't it? The news are that the Planets will trade for a new pitcher. The head coach as well as his players aren't sure that's the best move. I've heard that management are behind it." Luke chattered on.

The announcers were annoyed. Not only was Luke not speaking well, but he was also talking too much.

Watching the sportscast, the king was agitated. Why was Luke talking that way? He felt responsible for Luke hogging the microphone too. He may have done too well at prepping him.

"My father and I thinks the Planets doesn't need another pitcher," Luke said.

"Ugh!" the king exclaimed, exasperated. "Don't bring me into it," he mumbled. "My father and I thinks? Luke, don't talk like that. Luke clearly aren't nervous, so that aren't it." The king was talking to himself when he realized he was speaking funny too. "The Gremlin!" The king used his communicator to contact Kirk. "Kirk, there are a problem!" he said.

"I knows," Kirk answered.

"Find out what are happening on planet Sentence and quickly," the king ordered. He hoped there might be time to save Luke from any further embarrassment. At least Luke looked like he was having a good time.

Kirk and Ellen explained the task their father had given them to their mother. They left the media room for the castle library. There they asked Screen to give them a status report on planet Sentence. Soon footage of protests was produced.

"More protests?" Ellen groaned. "What do the signs says?"

"We won't be subject to anyone; no more subjection by verbs," Kirk replied.

"So subjects and verbs is having a disagreement this time?"

Kirk nodded. "The Gremlin are probably behind it."

Ellen pulled *The Guidebook to Grammar Galaxy* off the shelf and found an entry for "Subject-Verb Agreement."

Subject-Verb Agreement

For subjects and verbs to be in agreement in a sentence, both must be singular or both plural. Most singular verbs end in *s*. Recall that <u>is</u> is singular and <u>are</u> is plural.

<u>Use the following guidelines to make subjects and verbs agree:</u>
Sentences that begin with the word <u>there</u>, <u>here</u>, or <u>where</u> use the verb <u>is</u> with a singular subject that follows and <u>are</u> with a plural subject that follows.

There are 25 players on the Meteors' team.

There is a squirrel on the ballfield.

The contraction <u>doesn't</u> stands for <u>does</u> <u>not</u>. <u>Does</u> is a singular verb. The contraction <u>don't</u> stands for <u>do not</u>. <u>Do</u> is a plural verb.

The pitcher doesn't like the call.

The players don't like the call.

Compound subjects (two or more nouns or pronouns connected by the word <u>and</u>) use a plural verb.

The coach and his team take the field.

Singular nouns or pronouns connected by <u>or</u> or <u>nor</u> use a singular verb.

Neither the coach nor the catcher approaches the field.

Compound singular/plural subjects joined by <u>or</u> or <u>nor</u> agree with the subject closest to the verb.

The coach or some players run practice drills.

Some players or the coach runs practice drills.

Phrases between the subject and verb do not affect agreement of subject and verb.

The coach with several players approaches the mound.

Some subjects end in s (e.g., mathematics, civics, mumps) but require a singular verb.

The news is on.

Dollars may be singular or plural.

Ten dollars is the price of a spaceball ticket.

Dollars are taking up little space in the piggy bank.

Nouns like scissors, trousers, and shears that have two parts are plural.

Tweezers are helpful for removing splinters.

Collective nouns like team, family, class, and management are singular, but plural teams name use a plural verb.

The management is considering a trade.

The Los Angeles Lakers are on a winning streak.

"Those guidelines is a lot to remember," Ellen said.

"Right. Sort of. We will needs the guardians' help to get this mess sorted out," Kirk agreed.

"Another rally to get the subjects and verbs working together?" Ellen suggested.

"Not this time," Kirk said. "I has another idea." The two of them got to work on a new mission called "Subject-Verb Agreement." They knew they probably didn't have time to fix it before the game was over. But at least they could explain to the guardians why Luke was talking funny.

What does *exhorted* mean?

What is an example of something Luke said incorrectly?

What is one rule for subject-verb agreement?

Chapter 20

The Queen announced at breakfast that her sister Iseen would be coming for a visit in the near future. Ellen clapped and squealed with excitement. "We haven't seen Aunt Iseen in so long!"

"Have I met her?" Luke asked.

The queen laughed. "You have indeed met Aunt Iseen. But it's been a while."

"You don't seem excited about her visit," Kirk said. "Is everything all right?"

"Yes, yes," the queen said, but her response wasn't convincing.

Kirk and the king shared a glance as if to say both knew something was wrong. But neither mentioned it for fear of upsetting the queen. Both had forgotten the queen's negative reaction to her sister's impending visit by the time Iseen arrived.

"There they are!" Iseen exclaimed as she burst out of the space taxi's door. "Let me get a look at you," she said to her niece and nephews. "Kirk, you grew a foot! Ellen, you're as pretty as a picture. Luke, how dare you stop being my baby nephew! You're growing like a weed too."

Then Iseen turned her attention to the king and queen. "Sis! If you aren't a sight for sore eyes. Why am I getting older when you're not?" she said, embracing the queen warmly. "I still don't know how you snagged such a beauty," she said, winking at the king.

He laughed heartily. "Welcome back, Iseen," the king said, hugging her. "Let's get you settled in. We want to hear what you've been up to." He directed the butler to take her bags to their best guest room.

Later, Iseen joined the royal family in the sitting room. She entered with the enthusiasm of a fitness instructor. "What plans do we have for today? Where are we going?"

"Well, I was just thinking we would stay here," the queen said haltingly.

"Aw, your place is beautiful, Sis, but I was hoping we could live a little, know what I mean? Maybe go out for lunch?" Iseen pleaded.

"Oh," the queen responded, trying to cover her surprise. "I know Cook was looking forward to making some of your favorite dishes."

"That's 'cause she's my girl! I planned to eat more than I should. Know what I mean there, king?" she said, elbowing her brother-in-law.

The king laughed. "Unfortunately, I do!" he exclaimed, patting his belly.

"Don't you worry none, Sis. I'll eat whatever Cook whips up too. What's one of them fancier places you royals go? That's what I've been dreamin' of," Iseen said.

The queen began to make an excuse when Ellen exclaimed, "Mother, you have to take her to La Grammarille! It's so chic and even celebrities go there."

The queen tried unsuccessfully to mask a groan but recovered quickly. "Yes, it is indeed a fancy restaurant."

"That's just where I wanna go then. We can wait 'til tomorrow, though, so's I don't hurt Cook's feelin's. Now, Ellen, do you have any fancy new clothes to show me? I can't get over you girls and your outfits." Ellen nodded and led her aunt to her bedchamber.

The next day, the queen, Ellen, and her aunt Iseen took the space porter to La Grammarille for lunch. Ellen thought it was odd that her mother wanted to use the space porter. What was the rush in getting there, she wondered.

Her mother was acting funny at the restaurant too. She kept **scanning** the restaurant with a worried look. Aunt Iseen, meanwhile, seemed delighted by the restaurant's decor. She kept pointing out artwork that she thought was more funny than **sophisticated**.

★ ★ ★ ★ ★ ★ ★ ★ ★ ★

scanning – *looking over*

sophisticated – *classy*

★ ★ ★ ★ ★ ★ ★ ★ ★ ★

"Don't point!" the queen hissed angrily. Both her sister and daughter were taken aback. She quickly apologized. "I don't know what's come over me," she said, fanning herself with her menu. "Perhaps I'm ill and we should go."

114

Before Ellen or Iseen could respond, two women approached them. "Your Highness, I'm Abby from News Channel G. This is Eva," she said gesturing to the woman with a video camera. "If you're open to it, we would love to do a casual interview with you and your sister."

The queen **blanched** visibly. Iseen was giddy about it. "We would be happy to, wouldn't we, Sis?" Iseen gushed.

★ ★ ★ ★ ★ ★ ★ ★ ★

blanched – *became pale*

★ ★ ★ ★ ★ ★ ★ ★ ★

The reporter grinned, thrilled to have gotten the inside scoop. "Listen, we will keep it short. We don't want to ruin your lunch," she assured the three. "Let's start with why you're at La Gramarille."

"I love fancy restaurants. I had just came to the palace when I asked about going out," Iseen said, beaming. A blush of embarrassment began making its way up the queen's neck. "I haven't went anywhere this nice in years. But because I have the best sister anyone has ever saw," she said, side hugging the queen, "here we are!"

"Is La Grammarille your favorite restaurant, Your Highness? Is that why you brought your sister here?" the reporter asked.

"Ellen suggested it," the queen said curtly. "How much longer do you expect the interview to last?"

The reporter understood the queen's impatience and promised just a few more questions. "Iseen, what was your sister like when you were kids?" she asked.

"I have always knew I wasn't the smartest one in the family. That's my sister here. My sister has always took a book everywhere she gone. I'm so proud of her!" she said, side hugging the queen again.

When the three ladies returned to the castle, Iseen couldn't stop talking about the interview. It was scheduled for the news that evening. When the queen suggested Iseen go to her bedchamber to freshen up, she agreed. The queen then pulled the king aside and told him he had to immediately stop the interview from airing. "It was embarrassing!" she wailed. "She said, 'I haven't went anywhere this nice in years. I have the best sister anyone has ever saw.' Oh my stars! What will my friends think? And she will be teaching our children poor grammar too. Maybe I should make an excuse for why she has to leave," the queen thought aloud.

"Dear," the king said, embracing her, "before you make any rash decisions, let's have a family meeting." The king had all three children brought to the library where he and his wife joined them. He started the meeting by opening *The Guidebook to Grammar Galaxy* to the entry on Perfect Tense. He asked the queen to read it to them.

Perfect Tense
There are three perfect verb tenses showing the action is completed or perfected: present perfect, past perfect, and future perfect. The perfect tense uses the helping verbs **has**, **have**, or **had** plus the past participle. A past participle is a past tense form of a verb, usually ending in *-ed, -d, -t, -en,* or *–n.* The <u>present perfect tense</u> uses the helping verb *has* or *have.* It shows the action started in the past and continues to the present. The <u>past perfect tense</u> uses the helping verb *had.* It describes an action that happened before another action in the past. The <u>future perfect tense</u> uses the helping verbs *will have.* It describes the completion of an action at some time in the future. **Present Perfect Tense:** We have visited with our friend for a week. **Past Perfect Tense:** We had visited with our friend for a week before school started. **Future Perfect Tense:** We will have visited with our friend for a week by the time school starts. Irregular verbs cause the most difficulty in forming the perfect tense. Some common irregular past participles are listed below. be/been begin/begun bite/bitten blow/blown break/broken bring/brought choose/chosen come/come do/done drink/drunk drive/driven eat/eaten fall/fallen fly/flown forget/forgotten get/gotten (British – got) give/given go/gone grow/grown hide/hidden know/known lay/laid lie/lain ride/ridden ring/rung rise/risen see/seen show/shown sing/sung sink/sunk speak/spoken steal/stolen swim/swum sing/swung take/taken tear/torn throw/thrown wake/woken wear/worn write/written When in doubt of the past participle to use in forming the perfect tense, use the verb form ending in the /n/ sound if there is one.

Incorrect Past Tense: I seen.
Correct Past Tense: I saw.
Incorrect Past Perfect Tense: I have saw.
Correct Past Perfect Tense: I have seen.

"Why are you telling us about the perfect tense?" Luke asked. "Is the Gremlin up to something?"

"I bet he is. I heard Aunt Iseen use the wrong past participle at lunch today," Ellen added.

"No, children," the queen said sadly. "I'm afraid this is how your aunt talks all the time."

"Hasn't she read the guidebook? Should we go get her?" Luke asked.

"No, Luke. There are some things more important than good grammar and your aunt's feelings are one of them. Aunt Iseen isn't perfect, but we love her, don't we?" the king asked, looking to the queen first. Her face gave away her remorse and she nodded.

The children readily agreed. "All right then," the king said. "I have another lesson for you that isn't in the guidebook. It is impolite to correct others' grammar."

"What?" Luke exclaimed. "You correct my grammar all the time!"

The king laughed and even the queen chuckled. "Yes we do," the king said. "We're your parents. Parents and teachers can correct grammar. But others should not. Is that clear?"

"Kirk and Ellen can't correct my grammar then?" Luke asked, grinning.

The king smiled at his son's persistence. "Because you're a guardian, your siblings are also allowed to correct your grammar."

"Shoot!" Luke complained.

"Although we will not correct Aunt Iseen's grammar, we do have a mission. Tonight the interview with her and your mother will be aired. We want the guardians to know how to use the perfect tense correctly. I want you three to send out a mission before the interview. Make sure the guardians also know it is rude to make fun of others' grammar."

Kirk, Luke, and Ellen started working on a mission called "Perfect Tense."

The queen buried her head in her husband's chest and cried. "I don't think the interview will be as bad as you fear," the king reassured her.

"That isn't why I'm crying," she answered, sniffling. "I forgot myself. I love my sister. That's what matters. Thanks for reminding me." The king hugged her tight and suggested they find Iseen and see if she wanted to take a walk with them.

What does *blanched* mean?

Which helping verbs form the perfect tense?

Why did the queen change her mind about getting her sister to leave?

Chapter 21

"Father, you won't believe it," Luke said one weekend afternoon. "There's a new ride at King's Island."

"That's nice," the king said, focused on his newspaper.

"It's the highest roller coaster in the galaxy!" Luke explained.

"You don't say," the king mumbled.

Exasperated, Luke tried to gain his father's attention. "Didn't you like roller coasters when you were my age?"

The king looked up and smiled. "Yes, Luke, I did. Tell me about the coaster."

Luke sat down next to him. "It's called the **Terminator**. My friend's father designed it. It's not only the

★ ★ ★ ★ ★ ★ ★ ★ ★

terminator – *killer*

★ ★ ★ ★ ★ ★ ★ ★ ★

119

highest roller coaster in the galaxy; it's also the first rider-controlled coaster."

"Rider-controlled?"

"Yes! You can use your voice to control the speed."

"That does sound pretty amazing," the king admitted.

"Yes, and guess what?" Luke asked. He didn't wait for his father to respond. "My friend's father wants us to be the first to ride it!" Luke was so excited he was bouncing on his chair.

"All of us?" the king asked, touching his chest.

"No," Luke laughed. "Just us kids."

"Oh, that makes sense," the king said. "I don't think your mother is a fan of roller coasters anyway."

A few days later, the king reported to the family at dinner that Luke's friend's father had contacted him. A date had been set for the children to ride the Terminator. "There's one catch," he told them. "News reporters will be there filming your first ride. So you'll want to avoid being sick or chickening out last minute," he teased them.

The three English children laughed. "We won't do that, Father," they said in chorus.

"I'm going to go so fast!" Luke bragged.

"Will I be able to control the speed too?" Ellen asked cautiously.

"As I understand it, only one of us can control the speed at a time," Kirk said. "I've been reading up on it."

Ellen looked nervous. "As long as I can have a turn at controlling it, I'm willing to try."

"I can't wait!" Luke exclaimed. He shot his arms into the air and emitted a practice scream. The rest of the family laughed.

On the scheduled day, the family stood in front of the ride, smiling for the cameras. Ellen nervously surveyed the height and loops of the coaster. Kirk silently congratulated himself on having a light breakfast.

When they were allowed into the car, Luke eagerly examined the screen affixed to the front. It was similar to the screens the English family had throughout their home.

The three waved to their parents, reporters, and bystanders. "Have fun!" people in the crowd called to them.

"We will!" Luke answered.

"Welcome Your Majesties," the screen said to them.

"How polite!" Ellen said, trying to distract yourself.

"My wish is your command," the screen told the three.

"Go slow!" Ellen blurted out.

Nothing happened. Luke smirked at her. "She means go real fast," Luke said, snickering. The coaster didn't respond. Luke looked to his father worriedly. "Start?" Kirk suggested hopefully. The coaster **lurched** in response and raced up the first incline of the track.

★ ★ ★ ★ ★ ★ ★ ★ ★

lurched – *jerked forward*

inversion – *upside down*

★ ★ ★ ★ ★ ★ ★ ★ ★

"Go slow!" Ellen screamed to no effect.

"I like it," Luke said, laughing.

"Stop!" Ellen yelled.

The coaster stopped at the top of the lift hill.

"I like stop. Stop is good," she said, out of breath.

"We can't stay up here, Ellen. Start!" Kirk called out.

"Start slow!" Ellen called out.

The coaster raced into its first drop. "Airtime!" Luke shrieked with excitement.

"Go slow, go slow, go slow," Ellen chanted with no response from the car other than continued speed. The car completed its first **inversion** loop and slowed.

The screen then asked the three how the ride was going. "It's not going good," Ellen said, gasping. The car picked up speed. On the screen, the three could see numerous loops coming up on the track.

Kirk began to wonder if he would be able to hold on to even his small breakfast if the car continued to have a mind of its own.

The car whipped around loop after loop. Even Luke began to feel ill. "Go slow!" he cried. "Real slow!" When the car's speed did not change, Luke tapped the screen. "I think it's broken!" As the three turned into another inversion loop, Luke cried, "Stop!" The three found themselves hanging upside down in the middle of the loop. Ellen couldn't decide which was more terrifying, the breakneck speed of the coaster or hanging upside down at a standstill at that height.

"Start slowly," Kirk commanded tentatively. The car gradually began to move out of the loop.

"It's working; it's working!" Ellen said, nearly tearful with relief. "That's right. Go slow," she said encouragingly. At that, the car picked up speed. "Stop! Stop!" she yelled in a panic. The car responded by coming to a sudden halt.

"What did you say to get it to go slow, Kirk?" Luke asked.

"Go slowly? No, that wasn't it," Kirk said, but the car responded by inching its way forward. "Hm. It seems to like the word *slowly*," he said hesitantly. When the speed didn't increase, he relaxed.

"Go real fast," Luke ordered. When there was no response, he said, "Go quickly?" like it was a question. The car gained speed.

"Okay, okay, slow down," Ellen said. But the car's speed remained steady.

"Go slowly," Kirk said, and their speed decreased. "Huh. It responds to slowly and quickly but not slow or fast," he said to himself. The coaster accelerated. "Oh, I said quickly," Kirk said out loud. Their speed increased again.

"Go slow!" Ellen cried again. "Slowly, slowly," she said, relieved when the car responded.

When their ride was complete and they met with the coaster's designer, Luke said, "I know why you call it the Terminator!" His friend's father and the crowd who heard him laughed.

"It looked like you were having trouble controlling the car," the designer said.

"Yes," Kirk agreed. "When we said go slow or go real fast, it wouldn't respond. It only worked with slowly or quickly."

"That's right," the designer said proudly. "I wanted to create a grammatically-correct coaster." He nodded to the king.

"Oh," the king said, looking serious. "I applaud your commitment to good grammar. Let's meet to discuss the commands you've programmed into the coaster, shall we?"

The designer readily agreed. The king used his communicator to ask Screen to arrange the meeting.

As the royal family made their way out of the amusement park, the king told his children how proud he was of them.

"What are you going to discuss with the designer, Father?" Kirk asked.

"The same thing I'm going to discuss with you three guardians when we get home. Adverb-Adjective Confusion. I believe that is what caused the problem with the coaster."

"The Gremlin confused the adverbs and adjectives?" Ellen asked. "No wonder that ride was so bad."

The king laughed. "In this case, I don't think it was the Gremlin. You'll see what I mean."

In the castle library, the king read the entry on Adjective-Adverb Confusion from *The Guidebook to Grammar Galaxy*.

Adjective-Adverb Confusion
Adjectives describe nouns and adverbs describe verbs, adjectives, and other adverbs. Some adjectives are so similar to their adverb counterparts that they are easily confused. For example: *This is an <u>easy</u> recipe. (adjective describing recipe)*   *You can make this recipe <u>easily</u>. (adverb describing make)*   Most adverbs end in –ly but some do not, such as *never, not, less, almost, more, very, always, well*.   A few adjectives end in –ly, such as *lovely, friendly, chilly, orderly, ugly,* and *likely*.   **Even more confusing are flat adverbs that can be used as adverbs or adjectives.** They include: *fast, slow, quick, hard, far, close, fine, straight,* and *deep*. Some flat adverbs like *slow* have an –ly form. But both adverb forms are correct, despite arguments to the contrary.   *Drive slow. (correct)*   *Drive slowly. (correct)*   **Good and well are commonly confused.** *Good* is always an adjective; *well* is usually an adverb but it can function as an *adjective*.   *I am doing good at this. (incorrect)*   *I am doing well at this. (correct)*   *Am* and *feel* are both linking verbs connecting adjectives to the subject *I* in these examples. When used with these linking verbs, *well* generally refers to physical health.   *I am good. (correct)*   *I am well. (correct)*   *I do not feel good. (correct)*   *I do not feel well. (correct)*   **Bad and badly are also frequently confused.** *Bad* is an adjective, so is used with the linking verb *feel*. *Badly* is an adverb usually used to describe an action.   *I feel bad. (correct)*   *I feel badly. (incorrect)*

> *I played bad. (incorrect)*
> *I played badly. (correct)*
> **Real and really are often confused.** *Real* is an adjective meaning authentic; *really* is an adverb meaning actually or very. *Real* is used as an adverb in casual conversation, but should not be used as an adverb in writing.
> *I am real excited. (incorrect)*
> *I really can't go. (correct)*

"I kept saying 'go slow' and the coaster wouldn't slow down," Ellen said.

"Yes, and I said 'go real fast' and that didn't work either," Luke said.

"Right, but when I said go slowly, it responded correctly," Kirk added.

"Many people believe that 'go slow' is grammatically incorrect when it isn't. Saying 'go real fast' is incorrect, but the coaster should respond to casual commands," the king explained.

"What are you going to do?" Kirk asked.

"I'm going to ask the coaster's designer to reprogram the commands."

"I couldn't be happier to hear that!" Ellen exclaimed.

The king laughed. "But you three also need to send out a mission on adjective-adverb confusion. The guardians need to know how to use adjectives and adverbs correctly. And I have another idea. I would like the guardians to write the commands they want the coaster to respond to. I think feedback from future riders will be better received than anything I say."

Kirk, Luke, and Ellen agreed to work on a mission right away. For once, Luke didn't insist on having a snack first.

What does *inversion* mean?

Is saying, "I feel badly for you" correct?

Why wouldn't Luke want to have a snack before sending out the mission?

Chapter 22

"Are you nervous?" the queen asked Ellen.

"No. I was nervous turning the drawing in," Ellen said, laughing. "I didn't think it was done."

"I know! I remember. And what did I tell you?"

"Finished is better than perfect."

"Right. Aren't you glad you submitted your drawing to the Galactic Art Competition even though it wasn't perfect?" the queen asked. When Ellen wasn't enthusiastic, the queen continued. "No one can enjoy an unfinished drawing that stays in your room. You have a responsibility to share your talent with the galaxy. It's a lovely drawing. And I happen to love the subject matter."

Ellen smiled sheepishly. "Thank you, Mother. I know you're right. It's just hard to think about being judged."

"Oh, it is! You put yourself into that drawing. No one likes to be critiqued. But critique can give us confidence and help us improve." Ellen nodded. "I just know I can't wait to take your drawing home and have it framed. I was thinking it would look wonderful in the library. What do you think?"

Ellen beamed. "May I help choose the mat and frame for it?" she asked.

"Of course! Now that you mention it, I will arrange for a professional framer to talk with us about the craft. Would you like that?"

"Very much," Ellen agreed.

After dinner, complete with Ellen's favorite dessert, the family dressed to attend the art competition awards. Ellen was wearing a new dress for the occasion that the king noticed. "You look **stunning** and more

★ ★ ★ ★ ★ ★ ★ ★ ★ ★

stunning – *gorgeous*

★ ★ ★ ★ ★ ★ ★ ★ ★ ★

like your mother than ever," he told her.

"Thank you, Father," Ellen said, hugging him.

"You're not nervous, are you?" Luke asked. "They're just going to decide if you have any artistic talent at all. Nothing to be nervous about."

Everyone laughed and Ellen playfully tousled Luke's hair.

The art competition was being held in the exhibition hall of the art museum. Once the English family had entered the hall, Ellen wanted to run to find her drawing. But she remained **discreet** and feigned interest in the other art on display.

★ ★ ★ ★ ★ ★ ★ ★ ★ ★

discreet – *unnoticeable*

brusquely – *gruffly*

★ ★ ★ ★ ★ ★ ★ ★ ★ ★

"Look!" Luke pointed and called out too loudly as he surveyed a sculpture.

"Mind your manners," the queen reminded him.

"It's ugly," Luke whispered.

The queen looked around them, afraid he had been heard. "Luke, the families of all of the artists are here. And you're insulting them. Control yourself, young man." She looked to the king for support, but he was grimacing.

"You don't like it either, but you aren't helping me teach your son good manners," she whispered to him.

"I don't even know what it is," the king said. "But what's worse is this award." He touched a medallion affixed to the sculpture that read "Creativist."

"Is creativist an art term?" the queen asked.

"Not that I'm aware of. I think the award is misspelled."

"Please don't do this on Ellen's night," the queen responded **brusquely**. "For once, stop thinking about grammar and spelling."

The king sighed. "Okay. Sorry. It just drives me a little crazy."

"I know. But it doesn't matter tonight," the queen said, taking his arm.

The family continued walking through the displays. Kirk stopped at a piece that looked like a combination of the Wright Brothers' plane and a bird. He called the rest of the family over to look at it.

"Captivatingest?" the king said, pointing to a medallion. I suppose that's an art term too?" He tried unsuccessfully to hide his disgust.

"You don't agree that it's captivating?" Kirk asked. "I can't stop looking at it."

"It is captivating. It's creative too. But there's no such thing as captivatingest," the king explained.

When Ellen began to look upset, the queen signaled to the king to stop.

"Well, then. Let's find your drawing, shall we, Ellen? You know it's a winner with me," the king said.

"And me!" Luke added.

After making their way through the sculpture, multimedia, and painting entries, the royal family found the drawings. "These are incredible," Ellen said, breathless with awe.

"They're wonderful, Ellen. But these drawings don't make yours any less valuable. Yours is the only one I want to take home," the queen said encouragingly.

Ellen chuckled. "You're my mother."

"That doesn't mean I have no eye for art," the queen said, patting her daughter on the shoulder.

Ellen spied her drawing first and stood staring at it. Her drawing of Luke reading near a window seemed all new to her in this setting.

Luke broke her trance by exclaiming, "You got an award!"

"What?" Ellen asked.

"Yes! It says 'Most Bright New Artist.' Wow, Ellen! That's amazing!" Luke gushed.

Kirk congratulated Ellen as she continued staring at her drawing in disbelief.

An official from the art competition interrupted them. "Hello! You must be the artist. Congratulations!" he said, shaking Ellen's hand. "You have a talented young lady, Your Highnesses," he said with a slight bow to the king and queen. "You must be so proud."

"Oh, we are," the royal couple murmured in response.

"I'm so glad I caught you. We are photographing all the award winners with their work." He withdrew his communicator from his belt and was about to use it when the king stopped him.

"Would you please excuse us for a moment?" the king asked politely.

"Certainly," the official said graciously.

The king motioned for his family members to follow him away from the exhibits. "I won't let you take a photograph with that award," he said when they were gathered around him.

"What?" the queen exclaimed. "I thought we discussed this—" the queen began.

"This isn't about my need for perfect grammar. The Gremlin has to be involved and I won't pretend nothing is wrong."

Ellen's eyes welled up with tears and the king was immediately sorry for disappointing her.

"Ellen, I'm so proud of you. But guarding this galaxy is even more important than being photographed with an art award," he explained.

"Father, could Luke and I work on this? Perhaps we could solve the problem in time for Ellen to have her picture taken," Kirk suggested.

"I'm good with that!" Luke added.

"That's an excellent idea. I will stall the photographer," the king said.

"Will there be time to create new award medallions?" the queen worried aloud.

"I think I know how to handle that," the king assured her. "Boys, use the space porter to return to the castle. Look up Comparative Confusion in *The Guidebook to Grammar Galaxy*. Then figure out what the Gremlin's done to mess up the awards. When you know, send out a mission and ask the guardians to create new award medallions."

The boys quickly agreed and left. Once in the library, Kirk read the article on Comparative Confusion.

Comparative Confusion

Comparing two subjects is called a comparative and uses the word **more** or the suffix **–er** with an adjective.

He ran faster than his teammate in the 100-meter race.

Comparing more than two subjects is called a superlative and uses the word **most** or the suffix **–est** with an adjective.

He is the fastest sprinter on his team.

Add *-r* or *-st* to adjectives ending in e. For adjectives ending with one vowel and one consonant, double the consonant before adding *-er* or *-est*.

This cat is <u>nicer</u> than the other.

But the other cat is <u>bigger</u> than this one.

Some adjectives are irregular in forming the caparative or superlative. For example, good/better/best; old/older(elder)/oldest(eldest); bad/worse/worst; far/further(farther)/furthest(farthest).

Confusion occurs about when to use more/most vs. the suffix. Generally, when

---

the adjective is a single syllable, use –er or –est. Adjectives with two syllables use either -er/-est or more/most. When in doubt, use more/most. The ending *y* in an adjective changes to *i* before adding the suffix. With three or more syllables, always use *more/most*. Do not use both *more/most* and the suffix.

He is quicker than he was yesterday with his math facts. (correct)

He was the most gifted pianist of his time. (correct)

She was the happiest she had ever been. (correct)

He was the most fastest artist I've ever seen. (incorrect)

"What's a syllable again?" Luke asked when Kirk was done reading.

Kirk sighed. "It's the number of sounds or beats in a word. The word *helpful* has two beats—help-ful. Remember?"

"Yes, now I do. What did Ellen's award say again?"

"Most Bright New Artist," Kirk said.

"What's the adjective in that?" Luke asked.

"There are two. Bright and new."

"Right. Bright. New. Those have just one syllable, right?"

"Right."

"So they should use *–est*. Instead, Ellen's award uses Most."

"Right again."

"Now what do we do?"

"We figure out what the Gremlin's done this time. Screen," Kirk commanded, "give me a status update on Adjective Alley."

"Today in Adjective Alley," Screen responded, "is the first round of auditions for *Adjectives Have Got Talent.*"

"Cool!" Luke exclaimed. "I love talent shows."

"Not cool, Luke. I have a feeling the auditions are causing the problem. The first round is always terrible."

"That's true," Luke agreed.

The two used the space porter to leave for Adjective Alley. When they arrived, they found some disgruntled article adjectives. The adjectives weren't allowed to participate in the auditions. But they directed the boys to Adjective Theater where the auditions were being held. Kirk was able to get them both backstage by stating they were on official guardian business.

"It's so disorganized!" Luke exclaimed after observing the stage managers. There were multiples of *–er* and *–est* word endings being directed to join with adjectives. Multiple *more* and *most* words were also told to partner with adjectives as they left the stage.

"Excuse me," Kirk said to one of the managers. "How are you deciding which of these suffixes should be added to these adjectives?"

"We listen to the judges," the manager told him, gesturing to the people seated in front of the stage.

"I'll need to talk with them," Kirk said.

"We're on a very tight schedule. We're going to be here all night as it is," she argued.

"I understand, but it's urgent," he said.

The manager took Kirk and Luke out to the judges, apologizing. "These boys say they have to talk with you because it's urgent." She shrugged and returned backstage.

"Yes, it is. How are you deciding which adjectives should get *more*, *most*, *-er*, or *–est* added to them?" Kirk asked.

"Hey, we were told that we just had to give our opinion. This is the first round. Other people will get to vote later," one judge told him. The other two judges nodded.

"So you don't have any criteria like how many adjectives are in a category or how many syllables an adjective has?" Kirk asked.

"Nope," the judge answered impatiently. "The guy who hired us didn't give us any criteria."

"Who did hire you?" Kirk asked.

"It was some talent agency. I don't remember the name," he answered.

"I think we know who it was," Luke mumbled to Kirk.

"As guardians of the galaxy, we're going to have to insist that you use correct criteria for judging the adjectives," Kirk told the judges.

"Honestly, I don't need the hassle. I quit!" the first judge said. The other two judges grumbled their agreement and began gathering their things.

"Now what?" Luke asked, looking with alarm at the contestants still waiting to audition.

"We're going to ask the guardians for help. I'll get the list of adjectives auditioning from one of the stage managers. The guardians can help us judge," Kirk explained.

The two worked to send out an emergency mission called "Comparative Confusion." They hoped they could get new art award medallions done in time for Ellen's picture to be taken.

What does *stunning* mean in the story?

To use the suffixes *–er* or *–est,* how many syllables should an adjective have?

What should Ellen's award say?

Chapter 23

"**Preposterous**!" the king roared as he read his morning paper.

"What is it, dear?" the queen asked. She was used to him being upset when reading the paper. But he seemed particularly distressed. The children noticed too.

★ ★ ★ ★ ★ ★ ★ ★ ★

preposterous – *ridiculous*

★ ★ ★ ★ ★ ★ ★ ★ ★

"Parliament is considering cutting library funding." The rest of the family gasped. "That's right. Of all the ways they could save money, they choose this!" the king said, flicking the paper with the back of his hand.

"How much of a cut, dear?" the queen asked, hoping to minimize the problem.

"A thirty percent decrease. Can you believe it? They'll make it impossible for the library to buy new books and maintain their digital resources."

"So if they have a million pound budget, they'll be cutting 30,000 pounds?" Luke asked.

"I wish it were only 30,000 pounds, Luke. Try 300,000!" the king answered gravely.

"What are you going to do?" Ellen asked. "Can't you just order them not to make the cut?"

"That would certainly be justified in this case. But I don't have the power to create the budget."

"Can't you tell them what a huge mistake it would be to **decimate** the library budget?" Kirk asked.

"I can and I will. But they've heard about this from me many times. They think I'm too **sentimental** about libraries," the king explained.

★ ★ ★ ★ ★ ★ ★ ★ ★

decimate – *destroy*

sentimental – *emotional*

★ ★ ★ ★ ★ ★ ★ ★ ★

The children continued talking about the proposed library cuts and how it could affect them when the king interrupted. "That's it! Kirk, Parliament has heard from me about the value of libraries, but they haven't heard from you."

"Me? You want me to tell Parliament not to cut the library budget?" Kirk asked.

"Precisely! Who better to explain the impact of decreased funding than a young person who uses the library?" the king continued.

Kirk looked anxious. "So I would give a speech to Parliament? I don't know about that." Kirk felt like he was going to be sick.

"It's not really a speech, Kirk. You would give a written statement, yes. But the main thing is you would answer questions from the members," the king explained.

"That could be even worse!" Kirk exclaimed. "What if I don't know the answers?"

"I'll coach you. Besides, they know you're a young man. They won't expect you to know everything the head librarian does. I'll ask her to testify before Parliament as well."

"Are you sure I won't make things worse?" Kirk said, worrying aloud.

"I'm sure," the king said, smiling. "You just have to speak from the heart. I know you love our libraries. You don't want to see them fail."

"Why is Parliament considering such a big cut to libraries of all things? It doesn't make sense," Kirk said.

"It doesn't, does it?" the king added, thinking. After a moment, he said, "I have a feeling I know who has been lobbying Parliament for these cuts."

"The Gremlin," the rest of the family answered.

"Yes, the Gremlin. He must have hired a powerful lobbyist to get this cut under consideration. But we won't let it happen without a fight. Kirk, we need to get started right away. I'm going to contact the head librarian. We need to talk to her about the resources our libraries offer."

Kirk and the king met with the head librarian later that day. She felt the matter was just as urgent as the king did. The king had Kirk take notes on the services that the proposed cuts would affect. The two thanked the head librarian for the last-minute meeting and went home.

"I want you to write a paper that explains why you think cutting the library budget 30% is a bad idea," the king said. "Once you've written it, I'll help you edit it." Kirk nodded and got to work while the information was fresh.

Later that day Kirk finished the paper and took it to his father's office. The king read it, nodding and making notes. "Kirk, this is excellent! This galaxy is in good hands with you," he said, patting him on the back. "There are a few changes to make, but the most important thing is to be familiar with it. You can read it, but you'll be more effective if you can look up from the paper. You'll want to look these members in the eye. I dare them to take books from my boy!" he said passionately. "Well, then. I'm getting carried away," he said, clearing his throat. "I've already scheduled a time for you to testify."

"You have?" Kirk asked with alarm.

"Yes, next week. But you have plenty of time to prepare," the king encouraged him.

The day Kirk was scheduled to testify was nerve-wracking for him. He had practiced many times. He was dressed professionally too. But he had never testified before Parliament. The two had agreed that the king would not be present. He would watch the proceedings at home on TV with the rest of the family. The king wanted the focus to be on Kirk.

Once Kirk was seated, one of the members tried to put him at ease by explaining the process. The camera pointed at him didn't do anything to relax him.

When one of the members of the Budget Committee asked him to stand and speak, Kirk began reading his prepared testimony. The more he read, the more comfortable he felt.

"I could tell you all the things libraries do for the people of our galaxy, like provide free access to books, technology, education, and job training. Instead, I will tell you what the library does for me and my friends," Kirk said.

"My robotics club meets at the library. Without the library meeting room, we wouldn't not have a computer lab or space to meet that is convenient for everyone. Hardly none of my friends can afford the robotics software that the library makes available for free. Without proper funding, the library wouldn't do us no good. We wouldn't scarcely be able to compete as a team. That's after winning first place in the Galactic Robotics Competition."

Kirk looked up, beaming with pride at this last statement. The members of Parliament seated around him, however, were disgusted. The king, too, was appalled as he watched on TV. "This isn't not how your statement was written!" he cried. Then he gasped as he realized what he'd said. "Double negatives," he whispered. "No, no!"

The king grabbed Luke and Ellen. "You two have to come with me now!" He took them to the castle library and read the entry on double negatives from *The Guidebook to Grammar Galaxy*.

Double Negatives
A double negative is the use of more than one negative word or prefix in a subject-predicate set. Double negatives should usually be avoided in the English language. **Negative words include no, not (and the contraction n't), never, nothing, no one, nobody, hardly, scarcely, barely, rarely, regardless, and seldom.** *I can't get nobody on the phone. (incorrect)* *I can't get anyone on the phone. (correct)* *There is barely nothing left in the refrigerator. (incorrect)* *There is barely anything left in the refrigerator. (correct)*

Negatives are also formed using the prefixes un-, in-, non-, and ir-.
Irregardless of your schedule, we must attend the event. (incorrect)
Regardless of your schedule, we must attend the event. (correct)
In English, most cases of double negatives state the positive.
I can't go nowhere. (means I must go somewhere)
I never have nothing to do. (means I always have something to do)

"We haven't never seen this problem before, have we, Father?" Luke asked.

The king sighed. "No, no we haven't."

"I can't think of nothing we can do for Kirk," Ellen said sadly.

"It isn't never too late to do the right thing, irregardless of whether it helps Kirk," the king said. "Screen, give me a status update on planet Vocabulary."

"Why planet Vocabulary?" Ellen asked.

"I just haven't got no better idea of where to look first."

Ellen winced. Screen produced a news report from Word Immigration headquarters. The reporter described a new approach immigration was taking with newly-arrived words. "They call it the Buddy System," she said. "Words who arrive here no longer have to make it on planet Vocabulary alone." The video switched to an image of the words *not* and *nothing* leaving the immigration headquarters together. "Officials here hope the Buddy System will strengthen these words and the galaxy's vocabulary," she added.

"Did you see *not* and *nothing* as buddies?" Ellen asked.

"I did see them together and I think we have the source of the problem," the king said. "You guardians need to go to Word Immigration Headquarters immediately, or we won't have no money for our libraries. I'm going to go to Parliament and tell them Kirk has an emergency and will be back to testify later. First, send out a mission. You'll need the guardians' help to sort the buddies or we don't have no hope of a quick solution."

Luke and Ellen worked with Screen to send a "Double Negatives" mission to the guardians as soon as they could.

What does *preposterous* mean?

What are two negative words that shouldn't be used together?

Why is everyone saying double negatives?

Chapter 24

It was a chilly Saturday afternoon. The queen and Cook were settling on the media room sofa to watch *King of the Court*. The rest of the family weren't fans of the show, so the two had the room to themselves.

"I brought popcorn for us. I get nervous when I watch," Cook said.

The queen laughed. "Good idea," she answered.

The opening music for the show began playing. The **bailiff** ordered everyone to rise as the judge entered the courtroom. The host of the show described the **litigants** as they entered the courtroom.

★ ★ ★ ★ ★ ★ ★ ★ ★ ★

bailiff – *court officer*

litigants – *legal parties*

plaintiffs – *accusers*

★ ★ ★ ★ ★ ★ ★ ★ ★ ★

It sounded like a good case. A married couple was suing a plumber for water damage to their home.

The bailiff swore in the **plaintiffs** and defendant. The judge asked the plaintiffs to explain why they were suing the plumber.

"Your Honor, we needed a new toilet. Our old one kept getting clogged," the man said.

"It was embarrassing when we had people over," the woman added.

"They would be plunging the toilet, but it wouldn't work. They wouldn't want to come out of the bathroom, know what I mean?" the man said.

The queen and Cook giggled as did those in the courtroom.

"I ordered a new toilet that's supposed to flush better," the woman explained.

"I thought I could install it myself," the man said.

The judge spoke to his wife. "Ma'am, you rolled your eyes. What's that about?"

"I didn't think he could install it himself," she explained.

"I see," the judge continued. "Did you try to install it yourself?" he asked the man.

"Yes, and I had a little trouble," he admitted.

"Right! And you caused the water damage in your home, not me," the plumber yelled at him.

The judge told the defendant not to interrupt. "You'll have your turn," he said.

"So, did you hire this man to install your toilet when you had trouble?" the judge asked the plaintiff.

"Yes, Your Honor."

"Did he give, did he give—an estimate for the work?" the judge asked.

"He gave, he gave—his hourly rate," the woman said.

"Okay, did he tell, did he tell...how many hours it should take?" the judge asked.

"Did he tell, did he tell—how many hours it should take?" the woman repeated to her husband.

"Is the video skipping?" the queen asked Cook. "They're repeating themselves."

"I don't know," Cook said. "It's strange."

"He didn't tell—he didn't tell how many hours it should take," the man answered.

"Okay," the judge continued. "How many hours did it take?" he asked the defendant.

"You're asking—you're asking the wrong question," he said angrily.

"Let me ask—let me ask what happened," the judge said.

"I'll tell—I'll tell what happened!" the defendant cried.

"Not you, I'm asking...I'm asking what happened," the judge said, pointing to the plaintiffs. "Wait until I ask...wait until I ask what happened."

"You did ask what happened!" the defendant said defiantly.

"Sir, if I have to tell—if I have to tell to wait again, I'll have you thrown in jail!" the judge yelled.

"He must be really mad," Cook said. "I've never seen the judge stutter."

"What happened?" the judge asked the plaintiffs, looking exasperated.

"He removed the old toilet. After the new toilet was installed, it leaked. The water damaged the floor, the ceiling below it, and even our furniture," the man said. "I can give—I can give receipts for the repairs."

"I'll take those," the judge said. After he reviewed them for a few moments, he said, "You are seeking 4000 pounds in damages. Is that right?"

"Yes, Your Honor," the plaintiffs said in unison.

The king walked into the media room and quietly watched the show, without being detected by the two women.

"It's finally your turn to talk," the judge told the defendant, getting laughs from the audience.

"Your Honor, I did not install their new toilet. I went to the hardware store and bought—bought a new flange because their old one was broken. It's the part that allows the toilet to seal correctly. Anyway, when I returned from the store, they told...they told their plan to fix it themselves. If their toilet leaked, it's their own fault!"

The judge didn't have to ask the plaintiffs for their response. The woman was already saying, "He was charging...he was charging 125 pounds an hour. We paid—we paid that much to go to the hardware store?"

"Something's wrong," the king said.

The queen and Cook turned around. "Yes, it sounds like they didn't want to pay—didn't want to pay the money," the queen said.

"Just as I thought," the king said. "We have a problem too."

"Is our toilet leaking?" the queen asked.

"No. There are words missing. That's why everyone is stuttering," he explained.

"Which words?"

"It can't be direct. He charged 125 pounds an hour," the king said, talking to himself.

"Why can't you be direct, dear? The children aren't here," the queen said.

"No, I mean the problem can't be direct objects."

"Which objects? You mean that toilet flange he was talking about?" the queen asked.

The king sighed. "I'm going to get the three children. I'm going to give—to give a mission."

The king found Kirk, Luke, and Ellen in the kitchen, helping themselves to the rest of the popcorn Cook had made. Comet was happily gobbling up pieces they dropped on the floor.

"I am giving—giving news," the king said.

"News?" Kirk asked.

"Yes. Oh good grammar, just come with me to the library, will you?" the king said in frustration.

Once the four arrived in the library, the king found an entry for indirect objects in *The Guidebook to Grammar Galaxy*. He read it aloud to them.

Indirect Objects

An indirect object is a noun or noun phrase affected by the action of a transitive verb but is not the main recipient of the action. Indirect objects come between the verb and the direct object.

To find the direct object, ask who or what after the transitive verb. To find the indirect object, ask who or what got the direct object.

She gave him the book.

She gave what? book (direct object) Who got the book? him (indirect object)

"Is there a problem with indirect objects, Father?" Kirk asked.

"Yes. It's why I can't tell—tell what happened," the king said.

"What did happen?" Luke asked.

"I was watching *King of the Court* with your mother and Cook," the king began.

"I thought you didn't like that show because they use bad grammar," Ellen interjected.

"I don't. But that's not important!" the king said impatiently. "The people, including the judge, were stuttering like I am. I think they're missing indirect objects."

"Let's have Screen tell... tell what's going on," Kirk said.

"Yes!" the king said, relieved that his son understood.

"Screen, give—give a status update on planet Sentence, please," Kirk commanded.

Screen produced a list of search results for the planet. Nothing looked out of the ordinary, except one listing. Kirk tapped to open it and received this message: High-Security Password Required.

"What's the high-security password?" Kirk asked his father.

"I don't know. Maybe I stored it in my communicator. Give... give the high-security password," he said, speaking into his communicator. "No results found?" he said, incredulously. "I don't have a high-security password. I'm sure of it."

"Now what do we do?" Kirk asked.

"I'm going to call our head programmer to help."

When the programmer arrived, the king explained the problem.

"And you don't have a password?" the programmer asked.

"No. I don't remember creating one," the king answered. "Can you get into it without a password?"

"Possibly. I'll need to try from my computer."

The programmer left and was gone for what seemed like an eternity to the group waiting for him. He finally contacted the king via communicator. "Your Majesty, I'm sending... sending the information from the password-protected page now."

On the library's screen, a video began playing. "The galaxy's Witness Protection Program is designed to protect those who are indirectly involved in a crime. This page contains a database of the identities of those in the program. They must not be found. This information is top secret."

The king used his finger to scroll beneath the video. He gasped when he saw the list of words enrolled in the program. "There are indirect objects on this list. They don't belong in a witness protection program!"

"How can we get the indirect objects back?" Kirk asked.

"I'm going to contact the director of the GBI, for one," the king said. "I'm also going to need a list of all the indirect objects that should be released from the Witness Protection Program."

"We have a mission!" Luke said.

"You do indeed, Luke. Please send—please send a mission on indirect objects ASAP," the king said. "But tell—tell the need for secrecy! The guardians cannot reveal the identities of others in the Witness Protection Program."

The three guardians said they understood and got to work right away.

What does *plaintiff* mean?

What is the difference between a direct and indirect object?

Why were the people on *King of the Court* stuttering?

Chapter 25

"Today's the day!" Ellen squealed at breakfast.

"For what?" Luke asked.

Ellen was aghast. "For the Fanboys concert, of course. Who doesn't know the fanboys are playing tonight?" she said with great **disdain**.

"I didn't," Luke said, **oblivious** to his sister's insult.

"Ellen, not everyone is the music fan you are," the queen chided her.

"Everyone *should* be a fan of the Fanboys," Ellen said, defending herself.

★ ★ ★ ★ ★ ★ ★ ★ ★

disdain – *scorn*

oblivious– *clueless*

mournfully – *sadly*

★ ★ ★ ★ ★ ★ ★ ★ ★

"How much did we pay for those tickets?" the king asked. The queen avoided eye contact. "That's what I thought," he said **mournfully**. "Are you two going with anyone else?" he asked.

"Yes! The Grammar Girls and their mothers are going," Ellen said proudly.

"Grammar Girls? This concert is a Grammar Girls activity? It wasn't when I was a boy," the king complained.

"Dear, it will be fun for the girls. We can't be all write and no play," the queen said.

"I just know it's costing me money," the king complained.

"You're so generous with us, dear," the queen said, grinning. "The good news is we saved money buying group tickets."

"You're always saving me money," the king said, grinning back.

That evening, Ellen and the queen met with the other Grammar Girls and mothers outside the stadium's group entrance. Soon they were ushered to their seats. The girls chattered, looking forward to seeing their favorite singers come out. The women talked and laughed together too, enjoying their daughters' enthusiasm.

"Who's your favorite Fanboy?" Ellen asked her friends.

"I like So," one girl said. "He's so sassy," she said, resulting in giggles all around.

"I like Nor. He's kind of a rebel," another girl said. The rest of the girls murmured their agreement.

"Do you like this music?" the queen asked her friends.

"Not really," they admitted, laughing. "But it's something I can enjoy with my daughter."

The queen checked the time on her communicator and noted that the concert was late starting. Her friend noticed and said, "These things always start late. They're probably trying to get us to buy Fanboys stuff."

The queen relaxed and agreed. But it wasn't long before the girls started to complain. "How much longer?" they asked.

"Not much," one of the moms said. "I always tell my daughter that," she told the queen, laughing.

The queen laughed as well but was starting to get worried. She checked her communicator again. The concert was thirty minutes late. She wouldn't be able to keep the girls happy much longer.

Her thoughts were interrupted by an announcement. "Ladies and gentlemen..." At this, thousands of girls screamed. Their music idols were finally coming out on stage. "Due to unfortunate circumstances, the Fanboys will not be performing tonight. Your ticket payment will be refunded automatically. We do have Fanboys merchandise available for sale. After making your purchase, please make your way out of the stadium. Have a safe trip home!"

A loud chorus of boos echoed around the stadium. Ellen's eyes filled with tears. "They're not playing? We've looked forward to this for months!" she wailed.

"I know, dear. I'm sorry for the disappointment," the queen said. "B-, b-, however, we can make the best of it. Ladies, would you like to go out for ice cream?"

The group halfheartedly agreed, only to find themselves in an enormous line at the ice cream shop. The other attendees had had the same idea. "What do you think?" the queen asked the other moms.

"It's not worth it," one said. The others reluctantly agreed.

"Ellen, we're going home," the queen told her.

"Great! Just great. My whole evening is ruined," she complained.

"Do you want to stay a-, a- wait?" the queen asked her.

Ellen sighed. "No. I just wanted to do something fun."

"I understand, Ellen," her mother said, putting her arm around her daughter.

"Home so soon?" the king asked as they arrived at the castle.

"Don't ask," the queen warned with a serious look.

"What happened?" he asked.

"The Fanboys didn't play tonight."

"What. Why?"

"We don't know," the queen admitted. "We have a very disappointed daughter," she said as Ellen sulked and left for her bedchamber.

"I see that. Well, it's too late to do anything about it tonight. B-, b-, I'll look into it in the morning," the king said.

The king didn't have to look into it because the canceled concert was front page news. "I know why your Fanboys didn't appear," he told Ellen and the queen when they came to the dining room for breakfast. "Their coordinator is suspected of abducting them."

"Abducting them?" the queen said, astonished.

"Yes. Apparently, she met them at Conjunction Station years ago. She asked if she could be their coordinator. She managed to make them big stars. She was a bit too much of a fan and wanted to keep them to herself."

"B-, b- how could she abduct seven singers? Wouldn't she need help?" the queen asked.

"That's what the police think. A-, a-, there's more. Words are missing from the paper."

"S-, s-, it's a conspiracy?" the queen asked, frightened at the possibility.

"No. B-, b-, the Fanboys aren't who you think they are."

Ellen gasped. "What do you mean?"

"The Fanboys aren't just singers, n-, n- are they just musicians. They hold the English language together," the king explained.

"S-, s-, you're saying they're secret agents for the galaxy?" Ellen asked. "That's even more cool!"

"Technically, that would be 'even cooler.' B-, b-, the Fanboys aren't secret agents," the king said.

Luke walked into the dining room. "Why are you stuttering?" he asked.

"That's what I haven't explained. We are stuttering because of the missing Fanboys."

"The Fanboys are missing?" Luke asked.

Ellen expressed her impatience with Luke, but the king said he needed the explanation. When Kirk walked in a moment later, the king repeated the news about the abducted Fanboys. He called for *The Guidebook to Grammar Galaxy* to be brought to the dining room. He read the entry on coordinating conjunctions.

Coordinating Conjunctions

Coordinating conjunctions join words, phrases, and independent clauses. You can remember the seven coordinating conjunctions with the acronym **FANBOYS**:

for (because)
and (additionally)
nor (neither)
but (however)
or (alternatively)
yet (nevertheless)
so (result)

Coordinating conjunctions are preceded by a comma when joining two independent clauses (complete sentences).

---

*I did not take the trash out, **so** I will not be all to play video games. (two independent clauses joined by a comma)*

*I did not take the trash out **or** clean my room. (two phrases that don't require a comma)*

It is <u>not</u> incorrect to begin a sentence with a coordinating conjunction. Doing so can make long sentences shorter and easier to read. Beginning a sentence with a coordinating conjunction can also add a dramatic pause.

And then she told me I had to vacuum.

"S-, s-, the Fanboys really do hold the English language together," Ellen mused. "I'm an even bigger fan!"

"Yes, a-, a-, we have to get them back," the king said.

"How? Don't the police have to find them?" Kirk asked.

"The case has been turned over to the GBI," the king said. "B-, b-, the guardians can help look for them."

"You want us to send out a mission, a-, a-, you want us to do it right away. Right?" Luke asked.

"Right," the king answered.

"Okay. As soon as I eat breakfast. Cook will want us to eat while it's hot," Luke announced.

The king laughed and agreed. The three guardians began working on a mission called "Coordinating Conjunctions" as soon as they had finished breakfast.

What does *oblivious* mean?

When should coordinating conjunctions be preceded by a comma?

Why was the family stuttering?

Chapter 26

"Where are Kirk and Luke?" the king asked one evening after dinner.

"They're working on robots with Kirk's friend Leo," the queen answered, looking up from her tablet.

"Luke is with them? I didn't think Luke was into programming robots," the king said.

"Oh, you know how it is. Luke loves being included with the older boys."

"Yes, I know how it is. I also know it can be trouble," the king said.

"Trouble? The boys get along so well. You're worried about nothing," the queen reassured him.

The king decided to see what the boys were up to in the lab. They seemed to be getting along well. *The queen was right,* he thought to himself. He asked the boys if they had worked up an appetite for ice cream. They were happy to follow him to the kitchen for a treat.

The next day the king said goodbye to his family and used the spacecopter to visit planet Sentence. At breakfast, he had explained to the children that it was important he visit. It maintained good relations in the galaxy.

Ellen had plans to go shopping with a friend and her mother. The queen made sure the boys had something to occupy them too. Kirk and Luke said Leo was coming back over to do some more programming. That gave the queen some time alone to write.

In her study, the queen lost track of time. That often happened when her writing flowed. It was well past time for lunch, so she decided to ask the boys to join her. Before she reached the computer lab, she heard loud voices.

"Great! Just great!" she heard. It sounded like Leo and he sounded angry.

"Luke!" Kirk yelled.

Chapter 26: Interjections

"What?!" Luke yelled back.

Then she heard someone yelling, "Hey! Ouch! Stop!"

The queen rushed to the room. "Boys! Stop!" she ordered. Luke was on the floor and Leo stood over him, scowling. "What's going on?"

Leo yelled, "Luke broke my robot!"

"Did not!" Luke yelled back, rolling away from Leo.

"Did so!" Leo yelled.

"Wait!" the queen cried. "Kirk, tell me what happened."

Leo blurted out, "Luke broke my robot!"

"Did not!" Luke insisted.

"Did so!" Leo yelled again. Leo jumped onto Luke, attempting to pin him to the floor.

"Ow!" Luke yelled. "Help!"

"Now stop!" the queen ordered Leo. When both boys stood up, she asked, "Did you break the robot, Luke?"

"No!" he cried. "I promise!"

"Go! Get out!" Kirk yelled at Luke, pointing at the door.

"What? Why? I didn't do anything!" Luke answered.

"You wrecked my friend's robot. Ugh! You're never careful, Luke! Just go!" Kirk was furious. His mother had never seen him so angry. Luke started walking toward the door.

"Wait!" the queen cried. "Don't go! We need to resolve this conflict."

"Okay," Luke answered reluctantly. He stopped and walked back to his mother.

"Listen! We are going to settle this right now," the queen said.

"Great! You owe me for the robot you ruined," Leo said, pointing at Luke.

"Do not!" Luke yelled back.

"Enough!" the queen said. "Sit! Don't speak unless spoken to." When the queen could see that Leo was about to speak, she warned him to stay quiet with her eyes. "I can see that you disagree about what happened."

"Kirk and I agree about what happened," Leo said. Kirk nodded.

"I did not break your robot!" Luke shouted. The queen could see he was nearly in tears.

"Boys! Stop! We are going to come to an understanding," she said confidently.

"Right! As soon as he pays me for my robot," Leo said sullenly.

151

"Leo! Stop interrupting me," the queen warned. "Now then. Let's use the right-to-speak method. Leo, you're going to tell me what happened. Kirk and Luke, you will listen carefully without interrupting."

Leo explained that he had left his robot there overnight. When he returned, the robot wasn't working. Luke had been playing with it and had obviously broken it. The queen had to remind Luke not to interrupt.

"Now Luke. I'd like you to ask Leo three questions about what he just said that he can say yes to," the queen directed.

"How do you know I broke your robot?" Luke blurted out.

"No, Luke. He can't answer yes to that. Ask him a question that he can say yes to like 'Did you say that your robot wasn't working this morning?'"

Leo said yes. Luke sighed. "Did you say that you left your robot here last night?" he asked. When Leo said yes, Luke asked, "Did you say I was playing with your robot?" Leo said yes and the queen announced that Luke had three yeses.

"Luke, it's your turn to speak," the queen said.

"Finally!" Luke exclaimed. "Okay. First, I was playing with your robot while you were here yesterday. But I didn't play with it after you left. I didn't do anything to it! If it's not working, it's not my fault."

"Leo, now ask Luke three questions he can say yes to," the queen said.

"Liar!" Leo exclaimed.

"Leo! We do not call names. We will talk about name calling too. But right now I want you to ask three questions," the queen said firmly.

"Fine!" Leo said. "Did you say that you played with my robot yesterday?" he asked. When Luke said yes, he asked, "Did you say that you didn't know that you broke my robot?" he continued.

"No!" Luke responded.

"You'll have to ask another question, Leo," the queen said.

"Ugh! Did you say that you didn't play with my robot after I left?"
"Yes."

"Did you say that you didn't do anything to my robot?"
"Yes."

"Good!" the queen said.

"How did that help? My robot is still broken!" Leo said.

"You were able to make sure you understood what Luke was saying," the queen explained. "Kirk, did you see Luke playing with Leo's robot after he left?"

"Uh, no. I just assumed that he did," Kirk answered.

★ ★ ★ ★ ★ ★ ★ ★ ★ ★

assumptions – *expectations*

incensed – *angry*

★ ★ ★ ★ ★ ★ ★ ★ ★ ★

"Right. You assumed. **Assumptions** always cause conflict. Unless we observe something happen, we don't know that it did. We also never know what another person is thinking or feeling. If we assume that we know, we are likely to have conflict."

"You're kidding! So I just have to believe that he didn't break my robot?" Leo asked, **incensed**.

"Let me ask you, Leo, if there's any other explanation for your robot not working besides Luke breaking it," the queen said.

"No!" Leo said.

"Yes, there is," Kirk interjected. "My robot stops working all the time because of programming errors or because it's low on power," Kirk said a little sheepishly.

"Did you check your robot for those problems, Leo?" the queen asked.

"No," Leo said quietly.

"Let's check it right now, Leo," Kirk suggested. The boys soon discovered that the robot needed recharging.

"I'm sorry, Luke," Leo said. "I shouldn't have assumed you broke my robot," he said, looking at the queen.

The queen nodded and smiled as Luke accepted his apology.

"I'm so glad we've resolved this conflict. But there's something else we need to do to avoid these kinds of problems in the future. I'm going to create a kindness contract that I'll ask you to sign. Ellen, too. It will help you avoid unnecessary conflict in the future."

The queen went to her study to create the contract and decided to look for any news of the king. She was stunned by what she saw on the screen. "I'm here covering the king's visit to planet Sentence," a reporter began. "What was meant to be a public relations visit has turned into a public relations nightmare. Interjections are blocking

153

the royal procession. They are protesting that they aren't being treated like sentences. Earlier the king addressed the protesters," she said.

The broadcast switched to a clip of the king saying, "You are valued words on planet Sentence. But you are interjections, not sentences."

★ ★ ★ ★ ★ ★ ★ ★ ★ ★

dismayed – *distressed*

★ ★ ★ ★ ★ ★ ★ ★ ★ ★

The camera panned the crowd of interjections who were **dismayed**. They called out, "Oh! What? Hey!" and other expressions of disapproval.

"Oh no!" the queen gasped. "The Gremlin must have convinced the interjections that their rights are being violated. Hey! And that's why we're using so many interjections. Great grammar, I've got to get the guardians to work on this so their father can come home!"

The queen retrieved *The Guidebook to Grammar Galaxy* from the library and took it to the boys. She read them the entry on interjections.

Interjections

Interjections are expressions of strong emotion often followed by an exclamation point. They can be single words or phrases that stand alone or form a part of sentences. They are not grammatically related to the rest of the sentence.

Interjections may also be followed by a period, question mark, comma, or ellipsis. Some examples of interjections are:

Yeah! Great! Goodness gracious!

Well,

Um…

What? (when used to express disbelief)

There is disagreement about whether *yes* and *no* should be classified as interjections.

"Hey! We've been using a lot of interjections," Luke said.

"You're right, Luke. I think it's because of the interjection protest on planet Sentence," the queen said.

"The grammar experts have disagreements too," Leo noted. "They can't decide if *yes* and *no* are interjections."

The queen laughed. "Yes, it appears so," she said.

"Uh, I'm thinking we shouldn't waste any time getting an interjection mission sent out," Kirk said.

"I agree. Hey, Leo! Want to help us create a mission?" Luke asked.

"Sure! Cool!" he answered.

The queen showed the boys the kindness contract she had created. She explained that calling names and saying "you always" or "you never" could keep conflict going. Together they completed the contract and signed it. The queen suggested they include the contract and practice with conflict resolution in their mission.

The three boys agreed and began work on a mission called "Interjections."

The queen contacted the king via communicator to make sure he was safe.

What does *dismayed* mean?

What interjections did you read in the story?

What was happening on planet Sentence that led the boys to use a lot of interjections?

155

Unit IV: Adventures in Composition & Speaking

Chapter 27

The butler announced to the three English children, "Your tutor, Mr. Wordagi, is here."

The three of them knew enough to hide their chagrin that he had arrived. But Comet whined and ran away. *If only I could run away too,* Luke thought.

The students followed Mr. Wordagi dutifully to their castle classroom. "You are having a good day?" he asked them as he opened his briefcase.

Kirk, Luke, and Ellen said yes in a way that sounded like a groan.

"Good. Students, we are going to do something new," Mr. Wordagi announced. His **pupils** perked up. "You have mastered the art of copywork."

"Are we done with copywork?" Luke asked hopefully.

Mr. Wordagi chuckled but didn't answer. "Please get out your lined paper and a sharpened pencil," he ordered. "A mechanical pencil will **suffice**." He tapped the classroom screen and opened a file named Copywork. He then selected a paragraph.

"But you said we had mastered copywork!" Luke objected.

"I did indeed," Mr. Wordagi responded calmly. "Masters never stop practicing their craft."

"Ugh," Luke mumbled.

"Please copy this paragraph to your paper," he directed.

His three students began copying, knowing resistance was futile. They had complained about Mr. Wordagi before, and their father said he was the best writing instructor they could have. They resigned themselves to doing the work.

When Luke had finished copying his paragraph, he said, "Mr. Wordagi, you said we were going to do something new."

"I did say that, Master Luke. But I did not say we were doing something new *today*."

At lunch later that day, Luke discussed his theory on Mr. Wordagi with his siblings. "Mr. Wordagi wasn't working with the Gremlin when he started teaching us. But that doesn't mean the Gremlin hasn't gotten to him now," he said.

"He's still teaching us copywork, Luke. Nothing has changed," Kirk argued.

"Exactly. Why is he still teaching us copywork? He said we were going to do something new. Maybe the Gremlin hired him to drive us crazy!" Luke suggested.

"Luke has a point," Ellen told Kirk.

"If we tell Father that we think Mr. Wordagi is the Gremlin's accomplice again and we're wrong, Father won't trust our work as guardians," Kirk said.

"Kirk has a point too," Ellen admitted.

"I think we should have patience. 'He that can have patience can have what he will,'" Kirk said.

"Your copywork has gone to your brain, Kirk. I've been patient for a long time!" Luke complained.

"'Even waiting will end...if you can just wait long enough' – William Faulkner," Ellen said.

"You've been copywork brainwashed too!" Luke said.

Kirk and Ellen laughed.

Luke was not feeling patient during their next session with Mr. Wordagi. He put the exact same paragraph on the screen and asked them to copy it.

Luke sighed loudly. "Mr. Wordagi, when are we going to do something new?" he asked before beginning to work.

"He that can have patience..." Mr. Wordagi began.

"Can have what he will. Benjamin Franklin," Luke finished for him. "I am *not* having what I will!"

"You do not have patience, Master Luke," Mr. Wordagi said. "Complete the copywork."

The three students began copying the paragraph but were grumbling inwardly. When they were finished, Mr. Wordagi asked them for their papers. He tore them up and put them in the trash. Ellen gasped.

"Take out a new piece of lined paper," he ordered them. While they did so, he touched the screen and it went dark. "Now listen closely to me and write what I say."

Mr. Wordagi then read the paragraph they had just copied, phrase by phrase. The three students wrote quickly to keep up with him. When he was finished, Mr. Wordagi looked over each student's paper. "Good, good," he murmured. "You missed a comma here," he told Kirk. "Ellen, this word is misspelled. Erase and try again." He looked over Luke's paper. "Handwriting is hard to read."

"I know!" Luke said. "You read it too fast."

"You wrote too slowly," Mr. Wordagi corrected him. "Write faster." Luke frowned.

After class, Luke asked his siblings if they still thought Mr. Wordagi wasn't working with the Gremlin. "I don't know, Luke. I think Father will be angry if we bring that up again," Kirk said.

"Okay, okay. What if we don't mention the Gremlin. What if we say we think he should be fired? He's a dictator! He's making us write down what he says," Luke said. "Shouldn't Father know?"

"I think we need to wait, Luke. Maybe he made us write down what he said to punish us for our bad attitudes. I would hate for him to tell Father that we have been **insolent**. Then we will be punished again."

★ ★ ★ ★ ★ ★ ★ ★ ★ ★

insolent – *disrespectful*

★ ★ ★ ★ ★ ★ ★ ★ ★ ★

Luke wasn't happy but agreed to wait to talk to their father about Mr. Wordagi.

The next several sessions with Mr. Wordagi included more copywork and dictation. Luke was growing increasingly agitated. He hoped to convince his siblings to report Mr. Wordagi to the king.

Luke was in the kitchen with Cook after class one day, having a snack. He told her about how mean Mr. Wordagi was to them. Cook seemed sympathetic. "Luke," she said. "Would you do me a favor while we talk? I have to make a shopping list and my hands are all sticky. Use that pen and write these items on my notepad as I tell you."

"Okay," Luke agreed. Cook looked through her pantry and quickly called out a number of ingredients she was low on or out of. Luke added them to her list.

Cook looked at the list when she was finished and marveled. "Luke, I've never seen your handwriting look so good! I can actually read it. I was talking fast. I don't see anything misspelled either."

"Well, I...I've been working on it, I guess," Luke said.

"I don't suppose it would have anything to do with Mr. Wordagi's class," Cook said, smirking.

"I see what you're trying to do," Luke said, teasing her. "He's a dictator working with the Gremlin!" he said, chuckling.

"Obviously," Cook said, laughing.

Ellen had gone to find her mother. She was hoping to see if the queen was open to hearing some criticism of Mr. Wordagi. Perhaps she would take up their case with the king. The queen was in her office and when Ellen knocked, she was delighted.

"Come in, come in! I am so upset. My dictation software isn't working. I asked our programmer about it and he said I would have to contact the company. I messaged them and I got an automatic response. They'll respond in 48 hours. I can't wait that long! I have a mystery scene I need to write before it's gone. Could you take dictation for me?" the queen asked.

"Uh, you mean write down what you say?" Ellen clarified.

"Right. I'm used to saying 'comma' and 'period.' The only thing I'm worried about is talking too fast. I can speak quickly and my dictation software can keep up. Could we give it a try?" she pleaded.

"Sure," Ellen agreed.

The queen handed Ellen a notebook and pencil from her desk and began pacing. She began dictating to her daughter and Ellen wrote furiously. The queen seemed lost in the fictional world she was creating. Twenty minutes had gone by before she realized she needed to check Ellen's dictation.

"I'm so sorry, Ellen. I just get so caught up in it," the queen apologized.

"It's fine. What you wrote is very good, Mother," Ellen said smiling. She handed the notebook to her mother.

The queen began reading aloud what Ellen had written. When she looked up, her eyes were wide. "You kept up with me. How did you do that? And I can read it. And I don't see any misspellings. You're actually better than my dictation software!"

Ellen beamed with pride. "Practice I guess?" Ellen suggested.

"Well, whatever it is, you're a gem. Thank you so much, Ellen!" the queen said, hugging her daughter.

Ellen was interrupted by a call from Kirk on her communicator. He was contacting both her and Luke. "Meet me in the library," he said. "I'll explain when you get here."

When Luke and Ellen arrived, Kirk said, "Listen to this." He read them the entry on dictation in *The Guidebook to Grammar Galaxy*.

Dictation
The Latin root word *dict* means say. Dictation means to write what is said. Practicing dictation is a powerful exercise in improving spelling, grammar, and handwriting speed. To benefit from dictation, first copy the writing selection, taking note of spelling and punctuation. Then have someone read the selection to you, phrase by phrase, as you write it. Correct any errors.

"That's why I could write the shopping list," Luke said, thinking aloud.

"And it's why I was able to take dictation for Mother's novel," Ellen added.

"It seems Mr. Wordagi knows what he's doing," Kirk said.

"I do feel better about dictation," Luke admitted. "But there's something that would make me feel even better."

"What's that?" Kirk asked.

"I would like all the guardians to do dictation with us."

"That's an excellent idea, Luke," Kirk said.

"We could send out a dictation mission. That would make it fun," Ellen added.

Together the three of them dictated a mission called "Dictation." They asked Screen to deliver it to the grammar guardians.

What does *insolent* mean?

What is the difference between copywork and dictation?

What does dictation teach?

Chapter 28

"Mr. Wordagi has arrived for your lesson," the butler announced.

"Great!" Ellen replied, lacking enthusiasm.

"Ellen!" the queen said, chastising her. "He is the best writing tutor in the galaxy. And he takes time away from his own writing to teach you three. You should be grateful."

"I am, I am," Ellen said, unconvincingly. "I know copywork and dictation are improving my writing—"

"They certainly are," the queen interjected.

"It's just not that exciting."

"Learning isn't always exciting," the king added. "But it's like Dr. Seuss said, 'The more that you read, the more things you will know. The more that you learn—"

"The more places you'll go," Luke finished for him. "We wrote this for copywork. But we keep going to the same classroom every time," he joked.

The king laughed. "You children better not keep Mr. Wordagi waiting in that classroom. Know that I'm proud of you for working to improve as writers."

Kirk, Luke, and Ellen left the dining room and joined Mr. Wordagi in the classroom.

"You are having a good day?" he asked them.

When they nodded **glumly**, he said, "I have just the thing—writing exercises."

★ ★ ★ ★ ★ ★ ★ ★ ★ ★

glumly – *unhappily*

★ ★ ★ ★ ★ ★ ★ ★ ★ ★

The children groaned. *More copywork*, they thought.

Mr. Wordagi surprised them when he commanded, "Stand up! Now do ten jumping jacks." After the children completed them, he said, "Now do ten punches with each fist, like this." He demonstrated for them. "No do ten front kicks with each leg, like this." He kicked powerfully, high into the air.

Kirk, Luke, and Ellen followed his lead and were slightly breathless afterward. "Did Father hire you to teach us karate too?" Luke asked.

Mr. Wordagi laughed. "No, Master Luke. We do these exercises to get blood to our brain. It will improve your attitudes and help you think."

"I like it better than copywork!" Luke admitted.

"Your attitude needs more work," Mr. Wordagi said. "Read this," he said, putting a quote on the screen.

"In every job that must be done there is an element of fun. You find the fun, and the job's a game. P. L. Travers, *Mary Poppins*," Luke read aloud. "What's fun about copywork?" he asked afterward.

"That is what you must learn," Mr. Wordagi said mysteriously.

"Oh boy," Luke mumbled.

"Luke, you will tell me what is fun about copywork by next class," Mr. Wordagi stated as a fact. "All of you will copy this quote exactly," he said. Kirk and Ellen got to work immediately, wanting to avoid an extra assignment like Luke had received. Luke sighed and began working.

When they finished, Mr. Wordagi put more copywork on the screen for them to do. At the end of class, he handed each of them the dictation they had completed during the previous class. "I gave you feedback on your work. Please review it and be prepared to improve next week."

★ ★ ★ ★ ★ ★ ★ ★ ★ ★ ★

ulterior – *secret*

motive – *reason*

★ ★ ★ ★ ★ ★ ★ ★ ★ ★

The three students thanked their instructor and left the classroom. When they were out of Mr. Wordagi's hearing, Luke said, "So if he isn't working with the Gremlin, maybe he is just crazy. How am I supposed to make copywork fun? He's having us do kicking and punching. And I like that, but it's weird! And what do all these marks on my paper mean?"

Kirk hushed Luke, even though they were a distance from the classroom. "We have all become better writers because of being in his class."

"Okay, but maybe he has an **ulterior motive**. Like maybe he is trying to turn us to the dark side."

"You've been watching too many movies, Luke," Ellen said, shaking her head.

"Explain what these marks mean then," Luke said, pointing to his paper.

"I don't know. Maybe it's a foreign language," Ellen suggested.

"A foreign language? He's supposed to be teaching us English," Luke said indignantly.

"I don't think Mr. Wordagi is a native English speaker," Kirk said.

"What does that mean?" Luke asked.

"It means English isn't his first language," Kirk explained.

"He likes other languages better?" Luke asked, astonished.

"No. Mr. Wordagi is originally from planet Japan. He spoke Japanese before he came to planet English."

Luke gasped. "Does Father know?"

"Of course," Kirk scoffed. "It doesn't mean he isn't a good English teacher. His books are best sellers."

"Okay, but does Father know he is correcting our papers with Japanese?" he asked. When Kirk hesitated, Luke knew he had a point. "We aren't studying Japanese, so why should there be Japanese marks on our English papers? We need an English writing teacher."

Luke's siblings were quiet for a moment as they thought about what he'd said. Then Ellen said, "I would hate for him to be fired."

"He doesn't need the money, though, with all his book sales," Luke argued.

"But it would hurt his pride," Kirk said.

"He might be happy about it. I wouldn't want to teach me," Luke said. His brother and sister laughed.

"You have a point, Luke," Ellen said.

"Let's tell Father what is going on and he can decide whether to keep Mr. Wordagi," Kirk suggested. Luke and Ellen agreed this was a good plan.

Later that day, the three guardians found their father in his office. "Yes?" he said when he saw them. "This looks serious. Is something wrong in the galaxy?"

"No, this is personal," Ellen said. "It's hard to tell you this, but—"

"We're having a problem with Mr. Wordagi," Luke said in a rush.

"Not this again," the king groaned. "You admitted that his tutoring has improved your writing greatly!"

"It has," Kirk agreed. "But his behavior lately has been strange."

"And not very English!" Luke added.

The king frowned. "All right. Let's hear it. What has he done?"

"Well, he had us doing kicks and punches," Kirk said.

The king laughed. "Mr. Wordagi isn't just a writer. He has a black belt in Judo. I would love for him to teach me punching and kicking. Do you know how expensive martial arts lessons can be? He's teaching you for free. You better have something else."

"We do!" Luke said. "Kirk told me that he isn't an aborigine English speaker."

"What? That doesn't make any sense. An aborigine is someone who was first to live on planet Australia," the king said.

"I told you he wasn't a native English speaker. I didn't say he was an aborigine," Kirk said, annoyed with his brother.

"I thought that was the same thing. Anyway, he speaks Japanese, right?" Luke asked.

"Yes. He is multilingual. He speaks English, Japanese, and Chinese too," the king said.

"Okay, but why," Luke said as he dramatically handed his paper to the king, "is he using Japanese to correct our papers?"

The king took the paper, looked it, and erupted in laughter. "You think this is Japanese?" He laughed so hard that tears were forming in the corners of his eyes.

"What's so funny?" Luke asked.

"These are proofreading marks. It's not Japanese," the king said, laughing some more.

"Oh," Luke said somberly. "What are proofreading marks?"

The king looked concerned. "I didn't realize you didn't know proofreading marks. Kirk, Ellen? Do you know what proofreading marks are?" When both shook their heads, the king said, "I'm going to take you three to the library and teach you what these symbols mean."

Once in the castle library, the king read them the proofreading entry from *The Guidebook to Grammar Galaxy*.

Proofreading
Proofreading is carefully checking writing for grammar, spelling, and typing errors (also known as typos).
Wait some time before editing and proofreading your own work. Reading a paper aloud can help you notice errors. Having someone else proofread your work is also a good idea.
You or your proofreader will use marks to show changes that need to be made. Review the most common marks in the following chart.

Mark	Meaning	Mark	Meaning
 ℓ	delete	⌹	new paragraph
☰	capitalize	/	make lower case
∧	insert	 ∧,	insert comma
#	add space	 ⌣	close gap
⊙	add period	 ∿	transpose (trade places)
~~word~~	replace	sp	spelling error

The three children looked over the king's shoulder at the marks in the chart. "That's some of the Japanese writing that was on my paper," Luke cried.

167

"Luke, they are proofreading marks, not Japanese," the king corrected him. "Weren't you listening?"

"Yes! I mean those are the marks I *thought* were Japanese," Luke said. "I have a lot of those add space thingies."

"That's because you don't put enough space between your words," Ellen scolded him.

"Let me guess, you're not going to fire Mr. Wordagi," Luke said.

"Fire him? Don't be ridiculous. Once again he is teaching you three a critical skill I hadn't taught you. And you've given me a marvelous idea. I want Mr. Wordagi to help you send a mission to the guardians. I am going to contact him about it immediately," the king said.

Mr. Wordagi returned to the castle the next day and helped Kirk, Luke, and Ellen create a mission called "Proofreading."

What does *motive* mean?

Why did Mr. Wordagi have the English kids doing kicks and punches?

What does a proofreader mean when writing **sp** on a paper?

Chapter 29

The king and queen **lingered** in the media room one evening watching the news. Ellen had come into the room to ask for help with a math question. The next news story caught her attention and she watched silently.

★ ★ ★ ★ ★ ★ ★ ★ ★ ★

lingered – *dawdled*

★ ★ ★ ★ ★ ★ ★ ★ ★ ★

The newscaster described the controversy with wild horses on the plains of planet Composition as video clips of them played. "Planet Composition is dealing with overpopulation of wild horses. Officials say there isn't room for them as well as a growing population of sentences. One approach has been to use spacecopters to drive them to less crowded areas. A **domestication** program leading to adoption is another option. A few ranchers say the problem is so severe that they should be allowed to hunt the horses."

★ ★ ★ ★ ★ ★ ★ ★ ★ ★

domestication – *taming*

ardently – *passionately*

★ ★ ★ ★ ★ ★ ★ ★ ★ ★

At this, Ellen gasped. The king and queen turned around. "You aren't supposed to be watching the news, Ellen!" the queen chastised her.

Ellen continued to watch the newscaster say that animal rights activists were starting a Run Free campaign. They wanted the horses to continue roaming planet Composition as they had for years.

"They can't hunt them!" Ellen cried. "They have to run free. They're so beautiful. Did you see the babies, the foals? They're so cute! How could anyone kill them?" Ellen asked, near tears.

"And this is why we don't want you to watch the news," the king said, sighing.

"But isn't there something I can do to save the horses? I'm a guardian, aren't I? I should be able to guard the horses in our galaxy too," she said **ardently**.

"She does have a point," the queen said. "I like that she wants to get involved in political issues that are important to her."

"Politics isn't for children," the king said, disagreeing.

"Normally it isn't, but perhaps this time Ellen can make a difference," the queen responded.

"Please, Father? I can get my friends involved in the Run Free campaign. We can save the horses!" Ellen pleaded.

"I'm not sure that will solve the problem," the king said.

"They're horses, not problems," Ellen said, shocked that her father didn't appear to love the horses as much as she did.

The king sighed. "I can see that you feel strongly about this. I will give you permission to get involved." Ellen bounced on her toes gleefully. "But," the king warned. "I won't allow it to interfere with your studies or your duties as guardian. Is that understood?"

"Yes, Father. I promise it won't interfere. Thank you!" she said, kissing him on the cheek. "Night, Mother," she said, kissing the queen. She left the media room, forgetting about her math question.

The next morning at breakfast, Ellen couldn't stop talking about the wild horses. "I've already talked to the Grammar Girls about doing the Run Free campaign as our community service," she gushed.

"Already? How early were you communicating with them?" the queen asked, frowning.

"Don't worry, Mother. They were up. And they're as excited as I am!" Ellen said.

"Girls and horses," the queen said, smiling. "I loved them at your age too."

"It's front page news," the king said, holding up *The Grammar Gazette*. "That reminds me. Do you have a plan for getting the word out about Run Free?"

"We are going to make some posters," Ellen answered.

"That's a good idea," the queen said. "How about some brochures too?"

"What's a brochure?" Ellen asked.

"It's a page with writing on both sides that's folded in halves or thirds. It often has pictures too. In your case, it would explain what the Run Free campaign is about and why people should get involved," the queen explained.

"We have to have brochures then!" Ellen exclaimed.

"It sounds like a lot of work to me," Luke said.

"Horses are worth a lot of work," Ellen retorted, frowning. "In fact, the Grammar Guys should help us."

"We don't do horse stuff," Luke said, repulsed by the idea.

"But you write and this is writing," Ellen argued.

"We'll help you, El," Kirk said, smiling.

"You will?" Ellen said. Without waiting for a response, she jumped up and hugged her brother. Comet emerged from underneath the dining room table barking, wondering what all the excitement was about.

"I guess I'm helping too," Luke sighed.

"Thanks, Luke," Ellen said, laughing at her youngest brother's reluctance.

During the next several days, the guardians and their friends worked hard creating and putting up posters. The posters encouraged people to support wild horses' right to run free. The kids' communicators were constantly buzzing as they talked about the campaign with their friends.

Noting the excitement, the queen told her husband, "Isn't it wonderful how the children have taken up the cause? I'm so proud of them!"

"I'm proud of them for sure. But I'm worried. The horses have already been running free, and their large population is a continuing problem," the king said.

"I agree with Ellen. You can never have too many horses," the queen said.

The king held back, knowing his wife felt as strongly about the horses as his daughter.

After the family was seated for dinner, Ellen held up a brochure. "Our brochure is finished! One of the Grammar Girl moms works for a printer and had these printed for free. Don't they look fantastic?" she asked.

Her family agreed that they did. "Read it to us, dear," the queen encouraged her.

"Okay," she said, standing and clearing her throat. "Run Free is a campaign that seeks to protect wild horses of all breeds, including burros, and make sure they can roam the plains of planet Composition without fences or fear of being herded by spacecopter or being shot by hunters because wild horses are an icon of freedom that should not be limited by fences or greed or conflict and also because they are beautiful animals that do not destroy our environment the way some buildings and factories do so they should be protected the way our galactic parks are and like them be a source of pride and joy for all citizens of the galaxy as they are for Grammar Girls and Guys, who are sponsoring this campaign because they feel that as horses' freedom goes so goes our own that is worth fighting for that is worth contacting your member of Parliament for that is worth investing in by sending your payment to The Grammar Guys and Girls Foundation of the Galaxy that is worth putting a sign in your yard writing a letter to the editor wearing a Run Free t-shirt or even protesting with other Run Free campaigners on the dates and times we list below we thank you for caring about our wild horses." By the time Ellen finished, she was completely out of breath.

The king was wide-eyed at his daughter's long-winded reading. "Ellen, you and the Grammar Guys and Girls make many good points in your brochure it makes an emotional appeal and is likely to get many of our citizens involved to save the wild horses (and wild burros) from spacecopter herding and hunting by treating them like they are a national park (which I think is a clever comparison) because they are a part of our galaxy's heritage of freedom yet I'm concerned about how the brochure is written as it goes on and on and great grammar, I am doing the same thing!" the king exclaimed.

"What on English why are our sentences running on and on how did this happen, dear, do you think and what can we do to stop it, do you think it has anything to do with the Run Free campaign, do you think they're unrelated and most importantly what are you going to do about it, the children care about the horses yet we can't keep talking on and on and on like this, can we?" the queen asked, breathlessly.

The king looked angry. He called the butler and said, "Will you please bring *The Guidebook to Grammar Galaxy* to us, the book that has been in our family for centuries that has given us and our ancestors wisdom for ruling and protecting the galaxy from all sorts of trouble that the Gremlin, our arch enemy, thinks to stir up also our own foibles and so on—" The butler left the room as the king continued talking. The king was still talking when the butler returned with the book.

The king opened the guidebook and began reading the section on run-on sentences.

Run-On Sentences
A run-on sentence is an incorrect grammatical structure in which two or more independent clauses are joined without one of the following: a period, semicolon (;), or comma and coordinating conjunction. Run-on sentences are difficult to

read and confusing. Correct them by identifying the independent clauses (i.e. subject and predicate combinations). Then add a period, semicolon, or coordinating conjunction with a comma. A sentence following a newly added period must begin with a capital letter.

Birds migrate north and south they are usually seeking a better food supply. (run-on)

Birds migrate north and south. They are usually seeking a better food supply. (corrected with a period and a capitalized They)

A comma splice is one form of run-on sentence. A comma, rather than a period or semicolon, is used between independent clauses. To find many comma splices, look for a comma followed by the pronouns *he, she, it, we,* or *they.*

Birds migrate north and south, they are usually seeking a better food supply. (incorrect comma splice)

A semicolon may be used to join closely related sentences. The independent clause after the semicolon is not capitalized.

Birds migrate north and south; they are usually seeking a better food supply.

A comma, followed by a coordinating conjunction (for, and, nor, but, or, yet, so) can also be used to correct a run-on sentence.

Birds migrate north and south, and they are usually seeking a better food supply.

Grammatically correct sentences are also considered run-ons if too many independent clauses are connected.

Birds migrate north and south, and they migrate long distances, and they are usually seeking a better food supply, but some birds migrate for more daylight, and the daylight gives birds more time for mating. (run-on with too many coordinating conjunctions)

Ellen gasped and said. "We have run-on sentences in our brochure and we are talking in run-on sentences could this have anything to do with the horses I sure hope not that would be a disaster!"

"Screen, tell us what's happening on planet Composition we need to see if the Run Free campaign has anything to do with the run-on sentence problem we are having here it is driving us crazy," the king said.

Screen ignored the extra words the king said and produced a video that shocked the whole family. Protestors were kicking down fences on the plains. They were throwing periods and semicolons into piles while they chanted, "Run free!" Sentences and horses were running wild around the prairie while the protestors cheered.

"My word this is a disaster what are you going to do, dear, if you don't do something we will keep talking this way," the queen said, covering her mouth to keep from speaking.

"We need those periods and semicolons to control those sentences we need fences to keep the horses from destroying the grasslands that feed other animals native to the area I will send Grammar Patrol to keep the protestors from destroying fences and punctuation but you three need to send out a mission to the guardians called Run-On Sentences so we can solve this crisis."

Kirk, Luke, and Ellen understood the urgency and had Screen help them send out a mission.

What does *lingered* mean?

What is one way to correct a run-on sentence?

Why were run-on sentences increasing in the galaxy?

Chapter 30

Kirk found the king in his office working. The king said he was happy for the interruption and asked him what he needed.

"You know I just started Debate Club," Kirk said.

"Yes! I'm eager to hear how you like it," the king said. "I loved debate when I was your age."

"We are preparing for our first debate already," Kirk said. He grew pale and perspiration appeared on his upper lip.

"You're not nervous, are you, Kirk?" the king asked, a bit amused.

"Yes, a little," Kirk admitted.

"It's natural to have a case of the nerves for your first debate. Everyone in the club is likely to feel the same way. What topic are you debating first?"

"That's what I needed to talk to you about," Kirk said. "The topic is: Who is guilty of harassment, Wile E. Coyote or the Road Runner? Trouble is, I don't know who Wile E. Coyote is. And which road runner does he mean?"

The king laughed heartily. "My boy, we have to educate you right now. Screen," he commanded, "please play a Looney Tunes episode of Wile E. Coyote and the Road Runner."

"That is Wile E. Coyote and that is the Road Runner," the king explained as the characters appeared on the screen. Coyote immediately began chasing Road Runner with a knife and fork.

★ ★ ★ ★ ★ ★ ★ ★ ★ ★

reenactments – *imitations*

placate – *calm*

fauna – *wildlife*

★ ★ ★ ★ ★ ★ ★ ★ ★ ★

"It seems obvious who the harasser is," Kirk said, chuckling.

"Wait, just wait," the king said chuckling too.

"Meep, meep," Road Runner said, causing Coyote to forget that he had pulled the pin on a grenade that was still in his mouth. It exploded and left him covered in ashes.

"See, Road Runner messes with him," the king said laughing.

"I see that," Kirk said, laughing too. "We have to be prepared to argue both sides of the topic. So I will say that Road Runner harasses Coyote too."

"Of course he does. Why don't you keep watching this and take notes for your debate case? I'm going to get a workout in," the king said.

Kirk took his father's advice and took notes on the cartoon to prepare his cases. He started feeling less nervous and more excited about debating the case.

Kirk was fully prepared when it was time to debate in front of the club a week later. He asked to go first, so he could stop being anxious about it. His debate club coach flipped a coin to decide which case he would argue. He would try to convince his audience that the Coyote was the harasser. His opponent would make the case that the Road Runner was the true harasser.

Kirk made the first speech. He stood in the front of the room and began reading. He tried to look up from the paper as much as possible.

"Wile E. Coyote is guilty of harassing Road Runner. The definition of harassment is threatening someone. Coyote chased Road Runner with a knife and fork. He tried to kill him with an automatic boxing machine. He shot at him with a rocket-propelled arrow. He painted a fake road at the edge of a cliff. He swung a rock suspended by a rope. He placed explosives on the road. He connected explosives to giant springs. He placed a huge stone on a wood lever." Kirk stopped and waited for his opponent to cross-examine him.

His opponent seemed perplexed. "What is your definition of harassment again, please?" she asked.

"Uh, I said it's threatening someone," Kirk answered.

"Okay. I tried to follow your argument but I'm confused," Kirk's opponent said, looking helplessly at their coach.

"Yes, Kirk, I think we're all confused," the coach said. "The argument doesn't flow. We're going to have to work on it," he said.

Kirk sat down and his opponent was given her chance to argue that the Road Runner was guilty of harassment. "Coyote is not guilty of harassing Road Runner. In fact, Road Runner is guilty of harassing Wile E. Coyote. I want to expand on my opponent's definition of harassment. It is also annoying someone or putting them in fear for their safety. Road Runner appeared and said, 'Meep, meep.' Road Runner ran on a painted road. Coyote walked on the pained road and fell off a cliff. Road Runner ran through the Coyote's stop sign in front of the railroad tracks. Coyote is knocked onto the tracks and is hit by a train. Road Runner is on the caboose saying, 'Meep, meep' again." Kirk's opponent stopped and waited.

"Do you have some cross-examination questions, Kirk?" the coach asked.

"Yes, what is your definition of harassment?" he asked her.

"Uh, annoying someone. Or it's making them fearful for their safety," she answered.

"I don't know what else to ask," Kirk admitted.

"I can see why," their coach said. "There is no flow to her argument either. I'm going to let the other kids present their cases, but we need to work on these." Kirk's opponent frowned. Kirk understood her frustration. He felt it too.

After the rest of the club members debated, the coach said, "You're all just getting started. It's natural that your cases are **rudimentary**."

★ ★ ★ ★ ★ ★ ★ ★ ★ ★

rudimentary – *basic*

★ ★ ★ ★ ★ ★ ★ ★ ★ ★

"I think that means bad," Kirk's friend whispered to him. Kirk nodded.

"We have our work cut out for us, but we will improve!" the coach said, trying to encourage them.

That evening when Kirk returned home, the king met him, eager to hear how his debate went. "Which side did you argue?" the king asked him.

"I argued that Coyote was the harasser," Kirk answered.

"That's an easy win then," the king said, smiling.

"Our coach didn't seem to think so," Kirk said, looking discouraged.

"What do you mean? He didn't like your case?" the king asked.

"No. He didn't like it at all. The only thing that makes me feel better is that he didn't like any of our cases."

The king frowned. "Could I see your Coyote case?"

Kirk agreed, taking it from his backpack and handing it to his father.

The king read it silently, frowning.

"It's bad, isn't it?" Kirk asked fearfully.

The king sighed. "It's not bad...it's just—"

"You can tell me. The coach said it was rudimentary," Kirk said.

"I think we need help with this," the king said.

"Do you think I need more examples?" Kirk asked.

"No. Just come with me," the king said, leading him to his office.

Once in his office, the king asked Screen to give him a status report on planet Composition.

"Why are you checking on planet Composition?" Kirk asked. "Are you looking for Wile E. Coyote vs. Road Runner scripts?"

"No," the king said. "There's something missing from your debate case and I want to know why."

After a few minutes of the king scrolling through results, he displayed a video news report on the screen. "Here on planet Composition, these **transients** are being removed by the Grammar Patrol. They are accused of **loitering** in public places," the reporter said.

★ ★ ★ ★ ★ ★ ★ ★ ★ ★

transients – *bums*

loitering – *hanging around*

★ ★ ★ ★ ★ ★ ★ ★ ★ ★

Many words and phrases were being put into patrol vehicles and flown away.

"Where are they taking them?" Kirk asked.

"I don't know, but I have to find out. Kirk, this is a lot more serious than your debate case. Find your brother and sister and have them meet us in the library," the king said.

When the three guardians entered the castle library with Comet in tow, they found their father pacing.

"What is it?" Ellen asked.

"It has to be the Gremlin," the king said.

"Of course it is," Luke said, sighing. "What's he done this time?"

"He has Grammar Patrol rounding up important words and phrases on planet Composition and taking them to planet Recycling."

Ellen gasped. "Which words and phrases?" she asked.

"That's what I wanted to talk with you about. Ellen, read this entry for us, will you, please?" the king asked.

Ellen read the article on transition words her father was pointing out in *The Guidebook to Grammar Galaxy*.

Transition Words

Transition words are used to connect phrases, sentences, and ideas. Transition words make directions, reasoning, and arguments clear. Transition words can be used to:

add to what has been said: *in addition, also, together with, likewise, similarly*

show contrast: *on the contrary, unlike, while, however, although, despite*

describe causation or conditions: *if...then, when, so that, since, because of*

show results: *consequently, therefore, accordingly, for this reason, thus*

give examples or emphasis: *as an illustration, including, for instance, like, significantly, frequently*

give position: *opposite, beside, beyond, in the background*

show time sequence: *first, second, next, finally, suddenly, now that, henceforth, last.* Commas should follow sequence transition words.

Finally, allow the painted surface to dry.

conclude: *in conclusion, to summarize, overall, all in all, as I've shown*

Some transition words serve more than one purpose.

Transition words within a sentence such as *therefore, however, for instance, and for example* that introduce an independent clause should be preceded by a semicolon (;) and followed by a comma. When these words begin a sentence, they should simply be followed by a comma.

I agreed with her main argument; however, I questioned her on several points.

We eat a lot of produce. For instance, we have apples, oranges, carrots, and cucumbers daily.

"Without transition words, we will have a lot of confusion," Kirk concluded.

"Exactly!" the king declared. "This is why your debate case didn't work," he told Kirk.

"That makes sense!" Kirk said.

"We don't rescue the transition words from planet Recycling..." Ellen said.

"We can't say what will happen!" Luke added.

"I am going to get in touch with Grammar Patrol and have them stop harassing the transition words," the king said.

"We should send out a mission and ask the guardians to help us identify the transition words already removed," Kirk said.

His brother and sister agreed. They worked together to send out a "Transition Words" mission but found it frustrating with the missing words.

What does *loitering* mean?

What is an example of a time sequence transition word?

Why were transition words missing from the debate cases?

Chapter 31

The three English children took their seats in the theater near their friends. The seats were all taken by young people who were there to hear a speaker calling himself Mr. Possibility. Parents stood in the back, wanting to hear the famous motivator for themselves.

"We don't get any popcorn?" Luke complained.

"It's nine o'clock in the morning, Luke," Ellen reminded him.

"Oh yeah," he said, taking out his communicator.

"What are you doing?" Ellen asked. "You can't use that while we have a speaker," she reminded him. "You better turn it off."

"We could have a galactic emergency and we wouldn't know!" he argued.

Kirk laughed, overhearing the two of them.

The children in the audience quieted when the emcee walked up to the microphone on stage. "Good morning, young ladies and gentlemen! And good morning to those not quite as young in the back," he said. There were a few chuckles from the parents. "We have a real treat for you this morning. It is my pleasure to introduce Mr. Possibility. He is a best-selling author of more than a dozen books and audios. He is a wildly popular speaker, having taken his message of possibility thinking to CEOs, members of Parliament, and leaders across the galaxy. Today he will share his wisdom for life with you young leaders, who are our galaxy's hope and future. Please welcome Mr. Possibility!" he said, speaking directly into the microphone. He created a booming sound that **reverberated** around the room.

★ ★ ★ ★ ★ ★ ★ ★ ★ ★

reverberated – *echoed*

★ ★ ★ ★ ★ ★ ★ ★ ★ ★

The children stood and clapped as Mr. Possibility joined the emcee on stage. The emcee clapped him on the back and left while Mr. Possibility waited for the applause to die down. "Thank you, thank you," he said graciously. "I'd like to begin by playing a little game."

Luke grinned. He loved games.

"Let's say that your parents told you that in the morning you would go to Tomorrow Universe, our galaxy's newest theme park. Would that be all right?" he asked. "How many of you would want to go? Raise your hand," he said.

Mr. Possibility put a hand to his forehead to survey the crowd. "You all want to go. That's wonderful. You can put your hands down. You look like you're ready to go home and pack," he said chuckling. Some of the kids laughed and nodded.

"You want to go and experience Tomorrow Universe, but your parents have just one condition. You have to get your chores and school assignments for this week done by tomorrow morning. You have to get nearly a week's worth of work done today." A few children groaned. "Now don't worry. Your parents are going to help you. They will ask you everything you need to do to finish this week's responsibilities. And they will make a list of what has to be done. How many of you think you could get your work done in time to go on the trip?" Hands shot up around the theater.

"It looks like every one of you thinks you could do that! Okay. That's wonderful. My question is why don't you plan to go to

Tomorrow Universe every day? What I mean is, if you can do a week's worth of work in one day, why aren't you doing that now? What could you accomplish if you spent more time doing what matters?" he asked. A couple of the children raised their hands to answer. "That's a rhetorical question. That means it's something for you to think about." The parents in the back chuckled.

"Think about this," he continued. "With our hypothetical trip to Tomorrow Universe, you had three things that made it a possibility. You had a clear goal of a trip, you had a deadline, and you had a list of things that had to be done to reach your goal. With a goal, a date, and a to-do list, you can accomplish anything you set your mind to.

"Unfortunately," Mr. Possibility said, "your parents aren't taking you to Tomorrow Universe tomorrow. Unless I spoiled the surprise and that was your plan?" he quipped, looking to the parents in the back. They shook their heads no. "Young ladies and gentlemen, I'm sorry to inform you that your parents haven't planned a Tomorrow Universe trip for you. But here's the good news. You can decide where you want to go in life. What's your goal?" he asked them. "One thing I know for sure: you won't go anywhere if you don't have a goal."

Luke thought about what Mr. Possibility was saying as he gave examples of successful people. They succeeded because they had goals and worked hard. What should his goal be, he wondered. He wanted to be a leader like his father. *But how can I lead now?* he asked himself. By the time Mr. Possibility had left the stage and the audience was applauding, he knew. He was going to run for president of Grammar Guys.

Yes, he was one of the youngest members. But he had to think of the possibilities! He had to add attitude to his **aptitude** to achieve **altitude**, just as Mr. Possibility had said.

★ ★ ★ ★ ★ ★ ★ ★ ★ ★

aptitude – *talent*

altitude – *height*

★ ★ ★ ★ ★ ★ ★ ★ ★ ★

At home, the king asked the children and the queen about Mr. Possibility's presentation. "I so wish I could have attended," he said, "but I had an important meeting." The four of them told him how inspirational it was.

"And I have a goal!" Luke announced proudly. "I'm running for president of Grammar Guys." He was surprised by the look on his family's faces. "Mr. Possibility says if I can dream it, I can do it!"

"It's wonderful that you have a goal, Luke," his mother encouraged him.

"That is wonderful, son. I'm just not sure..." the king began before the queen hushed him.

"We are here to support you, Luke," the queen said, hugging him.

"We are too," Ellen said, pulling Kirk in to join the group hug.

Luke didn't have much time before the Grammar Guys election. He was a little discouraged when he saw several other campaign posters at the following Grammar Guys meeting. He posted his as well and said to himself, "If I can dream it, I can do it."

After the meeting, he handed out buttons his mother had helped him make. He noticed that most of the members were already wearing buttons for other candidates. "Where there's a will, there's a way," he said to himself as he walked home.

The election was held during the following meeting of Grammar Guys. Kirk encouraged him before the meeting. "You did an amazing job with your campaign with so little time, Luke."

"Thanks, Kirk," Luke said.

When the boys arrived at the meeting, the other candidates wished Luke good luck.

Later, as their Grammar Guys leader announced the results, Luke closed his eyes and tried to remember what Mr. Possibility had said. "The next president of Grammar Guys is..." the leader said. And it wasn't Luke.

Luke didn't hear anything Kirk said to encourage him on the way home. He had worked hard! And yet he hadn't won. Yes, he would have been the youngest president in the history of Grammar Guys. But he had believed it was possible.

The king didn't have to ask for the result. He hadn't expected Luke to win. "Luke, I'd like to meet with you in my office," he told him. Luke followed him to his office, shoulders slumped in defeat.

When they arrived, the king asked him to sit. "Luke, what is that saying of Mr. Possibility's you like so much?" he asked.

"If you can dream it, you can do it? That didn't turn out very well," Luke said.

"No, the other one about attitude."

"Oh, add attitude to your aptitude to achieve altitude?" Luke suggested.

"Yes, that's the one. You had a great attitude about this election. You believed in yourself and you worked hard. But I don't think you were using your aptitude," the king said.

"What do you mean?" Luke asked, suddenly interested.

"You're a leader as a guardian of this galaxy. But I don't think leading as a president of a group is your aptitude. Yes, you could do it. But your greatest talent is storytelling," the king explained.

"How can I add attitude to storytelling?" Luke asked.

"Mr. Possibility was telling you that you have to work hard on what you're good at. You're an excellent storyteller. But I can teach you how to be even better."

"You can?" Luke asked, intrigued.

"Yes. Come with me to the library. I want to show you something," the king said.

Once in the castle library, the king took *The Guidebook to Grammar Galaxy* from the shelf and read the entry on possibility thinking.

Possibility Thinking

Possibility thinking in creative writing is brainstorming or generating many ideas without criticism. The more ideas a writer thinks about, the more creative the ideas are likely to be. For example, instead of coming up with three space story ideas, come up with 30.

Ask yourself the following questions using the acronym SCAMPER* to create more possibilities:

What if I **substituted** something? (the ocean for space)

What if I **combined** something? (ninjas in space)

What if I **adapted** (changed) something? (a spacecraft that can also go underground)

What if I **magnified** something? (added another universe)

What if I **put** something to another use? (a robot that can also be flown)

What if I **eliminated** something? (spacecraft that battle without pilots)

What if I **rearranged** or **reversed** something? (the people think the hero is evil)

These questions can be used over and over again to create story ideas.

The SCAMPER acronym is based on the work of Alex Osborn and Bob Eberle.

"What if I used some of these story ideas with the kids at the library?" Luke thought aloud.

"Now that's possibility thinking!" the king said approvingly.

"And what if I lead the other guardians by sending them a mission about possibility thinking?" Luke suggested.

"Luke, that is a marvelous idea," the king said.

Luke worked on his own to send a new mission he called "Possibility Thinking."

What does *aptitude* mean?

What is possibility thinking in creative writing?

What aptitude of Luke's did the king encourage him to focus his possibility thinking on?

Chapter 32

Kirk, Luke, and Ellen returned from the main library branch on a chilly Saturday afternoon. It was a perfect day for reading. Kirk picked out a programming book, Luke checked out a joke book, and Ellen chose **contemporary** fiction.

Kirk wanted to use the coding instructions in his book right away. But he read it and reread it and couldn't figure it out. He decided to ask the head programmer for help. The programmer took the book from Kirk and perused it. "Kirk, this is a college textbook," he said chuckling. "You're not ready for this book."

Kirk thanked the programmer for his help. He was disappointed as he'd hoped to learn a new programming language that afternoon. He returned the book to his library bag and decided to work on his spacecraft model instead.

Luke was reading his joke book in the sunroom where the king was also reading. He laughed out loud several times until the king asked him to share what was so funny. When Luke read the line to his father, the king bolted out of his chair and took the book from Luke. "Luke! This is not a book for you. This isn't even a book for me," he warned him.

"It was at the library," Luke said, defending himself.

"I know and you're going to return it to the library," the king said. "Did you check out any other books?"

"Not today," Luke said.

"Then you can read one of the books we already have," the king said.

Luke sighed. "I'm going to play hide-and-seek with Comet instead."

"That's fine," the king said, returning to his own book.

Ellen found the queen in her office. "Are you busy?" she asked.

"Never too busy for you," the queen said, smiling. "What are you up to?"

"I'm reading this new novel I got at the library," Ellen said, holding up the book. "This beautiful woman meets this man who is soooo handsome that she can hardly speak to him—"

"Give me that!" the queen said, snatching the book from her. "This is a romance novel," the queen said. "You shouldn't be reading this!"

Ellen was confused by how upset her mother was. "Okay. I just thought it looked interesting. How old should I be before I read it?" Ellen asked.

The queen stuttered and blurted out, "Married! Ellen, listen, it just isn't for you. I'll make sure it gets returned to the library." The queen thought for a moment, feeling guilty about her reaction. "Are you hungry? Let's go make a snack."

Ellen readily agreed and accompanied her mother to the kitchen.

That evening as the family was being seated for dinner, the king said he had exciting news for the children. As their book selections had been disappointing, they were glad to hear it. "You three have been asked to do a presentation on perfect tense. Television executives for Channel G believe it's one of the more confusing aspects of grammar. They think you three can make it easy to understand," the king explained.

"Wow! We get our own show?" Luke exclaimed.

The king laughed. "You get one show," he corrected him. "You'll need to decide the best way to teach the concept. You need to plan and practice before they record the episode."

The three English children shared their enthusiasm about being on television throughout dinner. They immediately began planning their show after they were excused.

"I have an amazing idea!" Ellen said. "I think we should use puppets."

"Puppets?" Luke questioned, frowning at the idea. "Puppets are for babies."

"Kids love puppets and pay attention to them. And we need their attention to explain how to use the perfect tense."

"What kind of puppets?" Kirk asked.

"We have some alien puppets that would be just the thing!" Ellen explained. "We can have aliens landing on planet English. The king puppet can then explain perfect English to them."

"I'd like to be the alien puppet that says 'take me to your leader,'" Luke said, using a robotic voice.

"That would be great!" Ellen agreed.

"I was thinking that we could create a cool video to explain perfect tense," Kirk said.

"We could do that too. When the aliens see the king, he could play the video for them," Ellen said.

"I think we should include some explosions in the video so the aliens know they can't take over our planet without a fight," Luke said.

"Luke, they're puppets. They're not real aliens," Ellen said in a **patronizing** tone.

★ ★ ★ ★ ★ ★ ★ ★ ★ ★

patronizing – *superior*

★ ★ ★ ★ ★ ★ ★ ★ ★ ★

"I know. But real aliens could watch our show," Luke said seriously.

The three siblings began writing the script for the program.

The English children were nervous the day they were scheduled to record their show. The director seemed surprised that they had puppets. Ellen told her brothers that the director didn't know how creative they were. The director asked to review the video Kirk had put together. While the kids set up the props they planned to use, the director and her editors watched the video.

When the director returned to the set, she complimented Kirk on his editing. "It's clear you worked hard on it," she said. "My concern is..."

"What?" Kirk asked.

"Well, maybe it isn't a problem. Our audience will know that a kid produced it," she said, smiling encouragingly. "Are you ready for us to shoot?"

"Yes," Ellen answered. She handed the director a copy of the script and explained that the video would play immediately after their portion. Ellen had her brothers get behind the screen they'd created for the puppets.

When the director called "action!" the three followed the script and used the puppets just as they had practiced. When they were finished, the director looked **disoriented**.

★ ★ ★ ★ ★ ★ ★ ★ ★

disoriented – *confused*

★ ★ ★ ★ ★ ★ ★ ★ ★

"Is anything wrong?" Ellen asked.

"No," the director lied. The last thing she wanted to do was offend the king's kids. "Are you happy with that take?" she asked them.

"Yes!" Ellen answered readily.

"I didn't mess up any of the lines," Luke agreed.

"Okay then. I guess that's a wrap," the director said, looking to her editors incredulously.

"When will it air?" Kirk asked. "We want to be sure to tune in."

"We'll let you know. I'm not in charge of the schedule," the director said.

Several weeks later, the family gathered in the media room to watch their show. "It's on so late," the queen complained. "You children should be in bed. I'm only letting you stay up so you can see it live."

"Thank you, Mother," they said in chorus.

"I wouldn't think other children are awake at this hour, even to see this program," the king said.

The queen hushed him, so he wouldn't discourage the children.

"There we are!" Ellen squealed. The family sat wide eyed and quiet, watching the puppet show. Kirk's video that used a popular kids' song with cartoons played afterward. As the show ended, an advertisement for an area college ran.

The king sighed and shook his head.

"What's wrong?" Ellen asked her father, lip trembling. "You don't like it?"

"Oh, it isn't that. You three did an excellent job explaining the perfect tense. I can tell that you practiced a lot. But the audience is all wrong," he said.

When they seemed confused, the king asked that *The Guidebook to Grammar Galaxy* be brought to him. "This article on audience will explain what I mean," he said with the guidebook in hand.

191

Audience

Writers and speakers have to keep their audience, or the people who will read, listen to, or view their work, in mind.

Before writing, ask yourself the following questions about your audience:

How old is your audience?

Is your audience primarily male, female, or a mixture of each?

What does your audience need or what are they interested in?

How does your audience get information about your topic?

How much do they already know about your topic?

What opinions do they have on your topic?

The answers to these questions will help you inform, entertain, or persuade your audience.

"Your audience for your show is up late on a school night," the queen said.

"And the channel is advertising a college to the people watching," the king added.

"So I guess they aren't little kids," Ellen said.

"They won't like the puppets, that's for sure," Luke said.

"Or the cartoons in the video I made," Kirk said.

"I don't know about that, Kirk. Some older teens like cartoons," the king said.

"We wasted all that time on a show that teens won't like," Ellen said sadly.

"I'm hoping I can get the network to show this on Saturday morning," the king said. "I think it would be a hit."

"That's a wonderful idea, dear!" the queen said.

"I just thought of something," Luke said. "Remember that joke I read you a few weeks ago?"

"Don't remind me," the king said, groaning.

"That book wasn't written for a kid audience, right?" Luke asked.

"Right, Luke. You have to pay attention to audience when you're choosing books to read, movies to watch, and even music to listen to," the king said.

"That's why the book you checked out a few weeks ago wasn't appropriate, Ellen," the queen said. "Wrong audience. You three should stick to the juvenile section of the library or ask us if you aren't sure about a book."

"I asked our programmer about a coding book I checked out and he said it was a college textbook," Kirk said. "It was too high-level for me."

"That's a part of audience too. I'm glad you three learned something from doing this. It wasn't a waste of time at all. Now, it's time for my young audience to go to bed. In the morning, I would like you to send out a mission on audience to all the guardians."

Kirk, Luke, and Ellen agreed and said goodnight to their parents.

What does *contemporary* mean?

What are some questions writers should ask about their audience?

Why was the English kids' show a bad fit for their audience?

Chapter 33

"Today's the day you get to see a special screening of *The Secret Garden* movie. Are you excited?" the queen asked her three children.

"Yes!" Kirk, Luke, and Ellen agreed.

"Are they going to give us free popcorn?" Luke asked.

The queen frowned. "Luke, you are there to review the movie, not eat popcorn," she said.

"I think better when I eat popcorn," Luke said.

Kirk and Ellen laughed. "Mother, we do have a problem. We haven't written a movie review before."

"Oh, dear. That *is* a problem," the queen agreed. "Have you looked in *The Guidebook to Grammar Galaxy*? I'm sure there is information on how to write one there." The guardians admitted they hadn't looked. "I recommend you start there," their mother said.

★ ★ ★ ★ ★ ★ ★ ★ ★ ★

concise – *short*

entice – *lure*

★ ★ ★ ★ ★ ★ ★ ★ ★ ★

The children made their way to the castle library and Ellen read the entry on movie reviews.

Movie Reviews

A good movie review requires careful note-taking during the movie. You will want to have quotes and examples to support your opinion. You will need the title of the movie, the director's name, the lead actors' names, and the movie genre as well.

The review itself should have a title. The title of the review shares the main point of the review.

Everything is Awesome About *The Lego Movie*

Begin the review by capturing your reader's attention. Use an interesting fact, a comparison, or a **concise** opinion of the movie to **entice** the reader to continue.

If you created *The Lego Movie* at home, you would need more than 15 million legos!

The movie version of Louis Sachar's *Holes* follows the book closely.

If you choose to open your review with a comparison or fact, give your general opinion of the film next.

The creators of *The Lego Movie* have made it smart, funny, and a joy to watch. **Next, give a general plot summary without giving too much away.**

Stanley, a boy cursed with bad luck, is sent to a detention camp where he and the other boys are forced to dig holes.

Then, use the examples from your note-taking to give your opinion of the plot, the acting, and other features of the film (animation, videography, editing, music, costumes, and makeup).

The opening song, "Everything is Awesome," is so catchy that kids will be singing it for weeks.

Finally, write a summary of your review. Include an explanation of which viewers are likely to enjoy the film.

The best reason to watch *Holes* is Louis Sachar's story that appeals to kids and adults alike.

"That sounds simple enough," Kirk concluded.

"It does?" Luke said. "I thought it sounded like a lot of work."

"It's an honor to get to review this movie, Luke," Ellen said, correcting him.

"Every time I get an honor, it means I have to do something hard," Luke complained.

"Luke, we'll get to see it before anyone else. And everyone will be interested in our opinion," Ellen said.

"Okay," Luke agreed. "But what if we hate it? Do we have to write a positive review?"

"No," Kirk said. "The studio said we should give our honest opinion."

"That's good at least," Luke said.

The three guardians arrived at the theater later that day with notebooks and pens ready. The theater was dark, so it was hard to write. They did their best to take notes anyway.

Ellen had trouble getting into the movie while she was thinking about her review. Afterward, the boys admitted they had had the same problem.

"I wish I could watch it again," Kirk said. "I could write a better review."

"But we can't. Our review is due tomorrow. The newspaper wants to print it in time for opening weekend," Ellen said.

"I think we should get started on it right away then," Kirk said.

"Can't we wait to start until tomorrow?" Luke whined. "I'm tired."

"Luke, you've had enough problems because of **procrastinating**. We'll start when we get home," Kirk said firmly.

★ ★ ★ ★ ★ ★ ★ ★ ★ ★

procrastinating – *delaying*

★ ★ ★ ★ ★ ★ ★ ★ ★ ★

The English children referred to the guidebook as they wrote their review. Ellen was assigned to type it. When they were finished, Kirk ran an automatic spelling and grammar check. No errors were found. "Please send it to entertainment@grammargazette.com," Kirk asked Screen.

The next day, Kirk received a reply from the newspaper editor. "Wonderful job on the review, Your Highnesses!" it read. "If you would do us the honor of responding to the comments on your review at our website, we would be thrilled." The email went on to explain how to log in to the website when the review went live that afternoon.

"This will be so much fun!" Ellen said. Even Luke agreed that chatting with their readers online would be a good time.

As soon as the review was live, the three of them gathered in the media room. They asked Screen to refresh the website so they could see comments as soon as they were added. Ellen spotted the first comment. "Which garden was it?" she read aloud. "That makes no sense."

"This person wants to know what was secret about the garden we saw," Luke said.

"It's like they don't know *The Secret Garden* is a movie," Kirk said. "Wait! Did we say it was a movie review? Did *The Grammar Gazette* title it a movie review?" he asked.

Ellen used her finger to scroll to the top of their review and scanned everything on the screen. "I don't see 'movie review' anywhere. But isn't it obvious that's what it is?" she asked, feeling frustrated.

Luke asked Screen to refresh the website again. "There are more people asking for directions to the garden we saw. It's a movie!" he yelled at the screen.

"They can't hear you, Luke. We will reply to the comments that it's a movie opening in a theater near them today. That should solve the problem," Kirk said.

Their father entered the room and startled them when he spoke. "I see you've already learned the problem with your review."

"Yes, *The Grammar Gazette* didn't say that it was a movie review, and now everyone thinks we visited a garden. It should be obvious if they read the review!" Ellen explained.

"People rarely read everything in an article. And *The Grammar Gazette* isn't the only one at fault here. You didn't italicize the title of the movie or capitalize the title's main words. That's why everyone thinks you saw a real secret garden," the king said.

"I ran a spelling and grammar check," Kirk said defensively.

"Those checks don't pick up missing italics or capitalization. But the newspaper editor should have caught this. I'm going to contact the paper right now," he said, stepping into the hallway.

Momentarily, the three English children heard their father's voice rising in anger. "By whose authority?" they heard him ask. "There *isn't* a chair of the Department of the English Language. This policy will cause more serious problems than a confusing movie review," the king said.

When the king returned to the room, he explained what had happened. The paper had received a letter from someone claiming to be the chair of the Department of the English Language. The letter stated that italics would no longer be used for titles so Italian would be kept out of English.

"Are italics Italian?" Kirk asked the king.

"And what are italics?" Luke asked.

"I'm going to direct you three to look up titles in the guidebook. The Gremlin obviously sent this letter to create confusion. He's certainly succeeded. I have a big mess to sort out," the king said as he exited.

Kirk, Luke, and Ellen obeyed their father by heading to the library. Luke read the entry on titles aloud.

Titles

Titles of books, poems, movies, television shows, music albums, computer games, and other creative works must be set apart to prevent confusion. Capitalization sets titles apart. The two most common ways to capitalize titles are title case and sentence case.

In **title case**, the first, last, and major words (including proper nouns) of a sentence are capitalized.

Article adjectives (*a, an, the*); coordinating conjunctions (*for, and, nor, but, yet, so*); and short prepositions of fewer than four letters (*by, in, of, on, out, to, up*) are not capitalized in title case. Short verbs (is, are, am) <u>are</u> capitalized in title case.

Diary of a Wimpy Kid

The Name of This Book Is Secret

In **sentence case**, only the first word in a title and proper nouns are capitalized, just as in a sentence.

The invention of Hugo Cabret

When choosing title capitalization rules, use the case required by a teacher or publication and be consistent.

Titles can also be <u>underlined</u>, *italicized*, or "put in quotations" to set them apart. Italic is a print type, first used by an Italian printer, that slants to the right and is used to separate information. The general rule is that the titles of complete works are underlined in a handwritten document and italicized in a typed document. Parts of a larger work are set off by quotations.

> I read "Hiawatha's Childhood" in *101 Famous Poems*.
> We listened to "Do You Want to Build a Snowman?" on the *Frozen* album.

"You can title me *confused*," Luke said when he had finished reading.

"It seems that sentence case would be the easiest for titles," Kirk concluded.

"Yes, but even *The Guidebook to Grammar Galaxy* uses title case. I think all the books in this library do," Ellen observed.

"Good point, Ellen. We should have asked *The Grammar Gazette* which case to use. But with either title or sentence case, we should have capitalized the first word in the movie title," Kirk said.

"And the whole title should have been Italian, right?" Luke asked.

Kirk and Ellen stifled giggles. "In italics, Luke," Ellen corrected him. "But you're right that the title should have been separated from the rest of the text in our review. That way our readers might have understood that we saw a movie instead of a real secret garden."

"The guidebook would say that italics aren't Italian and can be used in the English language," Kirk added.

"Right!" Ellen agreed. "And even if they were Italian, we already know that English is made up of many foreign words."

"If I'm confused, I know the guardians must be. I think we should send out a mission," Luke said.

"That's a great idea, Luke. What if we have them write a movie review too? We learned a lot doing that," Ellen said.

Her brothers agreed, so the three English kids prepared a mission called "Titles." Afterward, they replied to more comments on their movie review, letting the guardians know a mission was on its way.

What does *procrastinating* mean?

What types of words aren't capitalized in title case?

Why was there confusion about the movie review?

Chapter 34

"Mail for you!" the butler announced, handing the three English children a letter.

Luke began opening the letter while Ellen urged him to be careful not to tear it. "It's written in cursive. You better read it, Ellen," Luke said after he'd opened it. "I can't read that as fast as print."

Ellen looked at the return address on the envelope. "It's from Ava Anderson." She glanced at the letter Luke held out to her. "Nice handwriting," she said, taking it from him.

"Dear guardians," Ellen read aloud. "I have a problem and I don't know what to do. First, I will tell you more about myself. I am a fellow guardian. Completing the missions you send out isn't hard for me. I love to read and write! But math? That is a struggle. I don't understand fractions at all. And I know why they call it long division. It takes me a very long time. I can spend all day on a few problems and still not get the right answers.

"My whole family is good at math. Everyone on this planet is good at math but me. I feel so dumb. I don't even want to look at my math. So I read and write instead. My parents are unhappy that I am not learning math. They say I have to know math to do well in school and life. I know you are grammar guardians and not math guardians. I hope you can help me anyway. Your guardian friend, Ava."

"I would feel dumb if I were bad at math too," Luke said sympathetically.

"I don't think that's what she needs to hear, Luke," Ellen said, frowning at him. "I know how she feels. Math hasn't been easy for me either. If you understand the lessons like you and Kirk do, that's great. But if you don't, you feel alone. No one talks about math in Grammar Galaxy. You're just supposed to get it," Ellen shared.

"I didn't know you weren't good at math," Kirk said.

"I know. I don't talk about it. It's embarrassing," Ellen admitted.

"It's okay, Ellen. If you're not good at math, Kirk and I can write Ava. We can explain fractions and long division to her. Then she can get her math work done and her parents will be proud!" Luke said.

"You don't get it, Luke," Ellen retorted. She took the letter and stormed off in the direction of her bedchamber.

"What's her problem?" Luke asked Kirk.

"A girl thing I guess?" Kirk suggested.

At dinner that evening, Luke mentioned Ava's letter. "This girl is really bad at math. She wants us to help her. Ellen said she is really bad at math too, so I said that Kirk and I could tell Ava how to do fractions and long division. Then she wouldn't feel so dumb. But Ellen was mad at me for saying that, for some reason."

Ellen **glowered** at Luke. "You are so insensitive!" she yelled at him.

★ ★ ★ ★ ★ ★ ★ ★ ★ ★

glowered – *glared*

★ ★ ★ ★ ★ ★ ★ ★ ★ ★

"Ellen! Don't raise your voice," her mother said, correcting her.

"I didn't realize you were bad at math," the king said.

The queen glared at her husband, warning him to change his approach. "What I mean is, I didn't realize this was a sensitive subject for you. I'm sure you aren't bad at math," the king said reassuringly.

"Math is hard for me. And it's really hard to have trouble with math when you live on planet English. No one talks about math. It's just English, English, English! I have to divide these fractions and I don't even know what that means. It seems like everyone understands it but me!" Ellen ranted.

"That's just what Ava said, so there are two of you who are bad at math," Luke said, trying to encourage his sister.

"Ugh!" Ellen exclaimed in frustration. She stood up abruptly and asked for permission to go to her bedchamber. When the queen agreed, Comet emerged from underneath the dining room table and trotted after her.

"She went to her room mad this afternoon too. Girls are weird," Luke said, expecting a chuckle. He didn't get one.

"Luke, that was not kind," his mother chided him.

"I was trying to tell her that she isn't the only one bad at math," Luke said, defending himself.

"Luke, I think the phrase 'bad at math' is getting you into trouble," the king explained.

"She's the one who said she's bad at math. I was just agreeing with her," Luke said.

"Never agree with a woman who says something negative about herself, Luke. I've learned that the hard way," the king said, grinning at his wife.

"Okay, but Ellen can't help Ava with her math. I said that Kirk and I could explain fractions and long division to her," Luke said.

"You're going to explain all of that in a letter? And your letter is going to help her understand math when nothing else has worked?" the king asked **dubiously**.

★ ★ ★ ★ ★ ★ ★ ★ ★ ★

dubiously – *doubtfully*

★ ★ ★ ★ ★ ★ ★ ★ ★ ★

"I wondered how that would help," Kirk admitted.

"If we don't tell her how to do math, what can we do for her? Nothing?" Luke asked.

The king pushed himself back from the table and stroked his beard. "I have an idea," he announced. "I want to share it with your sister first."

A few minutes later, the king quietly knocked on his daughter's bedchamber door.

"Come in," she said. "Unless you're Luke."

The king couldn't help but laugh. "Your brother hasn't learned how to talk to a girl when she's upset. But he means well," he said. He sat on the end of her bed. "I'm surprised you haven't mentioned your problem with math before."

"No one else seems to struggle with it. I don't want to feel like I'm stupid by saying anything," she said, her throat choked with emotion.

"What are you going to say to Ava?" the king asked.

"What do you mean?" Ellen replied.

"I mean, are you going to tell Ava you have the same problem?"

"I don't see how that will help," she said, sighing.

"It wouldn't help her do math, but it could help her feel like she's not alone," the king said softly.

"Yes. So there are two of us then, just like Luke said," she said, angry again.

The king put up his hands in mock surrender. "Ellen, there are more than two of you. We need to do a better job as a galaxy of talking about struggles we have. I can see where it would be hard to admit that you're having a tough time when no one else admits it." Ellen nodded, looking grateful for her father's understanding.

"I have an idea that I think can help all of us," the king said. He explained his plan as Ellen's mood brightened.

"I like it," she said, smiling. "I think I would be good at it."

"I think you will be too," the king said, returning her smile. "I'd like to have the boys meet us in the library to start preparing. Are you comfortable with that?"

Ellen nodded and hugged her father. The two of them went to find Kirk and Luke and were trailed by Comet. When they reached the castle library, the king asked Luke to read the entry on writing realistic fiction.

★ ★ ★ ★ ★ ★ ★ ★ ★ ★

relatable– *relevant*

★ ★ ★ ★ ★ ★ ★ ★ ★ ★

Writing Realistic Fiction

Realistic fiction is a literary genre made up of believable stories.

To write realistic fiction, first choose a story idea. Realistic fiction often teaches a life lesson. What realistic problem does your audience have that your story could solve? Brainstorm ideas and choose the story that is most **relatable**.

Second, choose a setting you know. A wilderness setting for your story will not be as realistic if you haven't experienced it. Make notes about the time, place, and mood of your story.

Third, develop believable characters. Describe any physical traits of your characters that are important to the story. Include character traits you see in yourself and people you know. This will make your characters more realistic.

Believable characters aren't flat but round. That means they demonstrate more than one or two traits or emotions and they change over time. An evil villain who doesn't care about anyone and doesn't change is a flat character. A villain who loves animals and changes his mind about his evil plan is a round character.

Fourth, create your story arc (rising action leading to a climax, falling action, and a resolution). You will add scenes or the major events that move the story along to the arc.

Fifth, write your story. Refer back to your notes as you write, but do not edit your first draft for grammar or spelling. If you get stuck, picture the story in your mind. What would your character do or say if it were a movie? Then write what you see happening.

Finally, edit your story. Read the story out loud to someone else. You'll notice problems with the story doing this that you would otherwise miss. Your listener can make suggestions. Correct spelling and grammar and ask someone to proofread it for you. You may add illustrations to the finished story if you wish.

"Why do you want us to write realistic fiction?" Luke asked when he was finished reading the entry.

"Because stories can inspire us, comfort us, and motivate us," the king answered.

"We can write a story about a girl who struggles with math and how she solves the problem," Ellen explained.

"But we don't know how to solve the problem, do we?" Luke asked.

"That's what you can research," the king suggested. "Screen can help."

"The guardians could help too," Kirk added.

"That's a splendid idea, Kirk. You can ask them how they have improved in a subject that doesn't come easily to them. I also think the guardians should know how to write realistic fiction. Don't you?" the king asked.

The three English children agreed and created a mission called "Writing Realistic Fiction."

What does *glowered* mean?

How is realistic fiction different from science fiction?

What is the difference between flat and round characters?

Chapter 35

"Summer is coming and it's already warm enough to swim!" Luke exclaimed at breakfast one Saturday morning.

"What's the high today?" Ellen asked Screen. When the answer was unseasonably warm, Ellen asked, "Can we swim today?"

"I don't see why not," her mother said, smiling. "I wonder if your bathing suits still fit."

"If not, we could go shopping," Ellen said hopefully.

The queen and Ellen did make a quick trip to the store to buy swimsuits and goggles for all three kids. The boys declined to go.

After they returned, the young guardians spent most of the day in the pool so that their fingers **resembled** prunes. The king liked that they were getting exercise. The queen was happy that the children were outside. Even Comet was happy, running around the **perimeter** of the pool barking as the kids swam.

★ ★ ★ ★ ★ ★ ★ ★ ★ ★

resembled – *looked like*

perimeter – *outside*

★ ★ ★ ★ ★ ★ ★ ★ ★ ★

The English kids repeated their pool time the next day. By the time summer had officially arrived, they were spending several hours daily in the pool.

Then one morning the king showed the queen an ad in the first section of *The Grammar Gazette*. Their three children were pictured in the royal swimming pool. The ad copy read, "Why waste your time reading this summer when even the royal guardians aren't spending time on boring books?!"

The queen gasped. "How did they get this picture?"

The king was upset for a different reason. "The children have been reading, haven't they?"

The queen stammered and then made it clear she wasn't sure.

★ ★ ★ ★ ★ ★ ★ ★ ★ ★

pronto – *quickly*

★ ★ ★ ★ ★ ★ ★ ★ ★ ★

The king asked the butler to bring Kirk, Luke, and Ellen to him **pronto**. The children came to him, still sleepy. The king showed them the ad. "I am all for swimming. It's great exercise. But have you three been reading?"

The guardians looked at one another sheepishly. The king grew alarmed. "What book are you reading now, Luke?"

"Uh, I have a book. The name of it is...I just can't remember now," Luke said, staring at his feet. "I just woke up."

"It doesn't matter, Luke. You've told me what I needed to know," the king said, disappointed. "This ad has likely had a negative impact on reading across the galaxy."

"Maybe more kids are swimming though?" Ellen suggested.

"Must I remind you of the consequences of an illiterate galaxy?" the king said more angrily than he intended.

Ellen shook her head, ashamed.

"I'm sorry," the king said when he noticed her reaction. "I know you've been having fun swimming this summer. But you and the rest of our young people must continue reading as well."

"We will, Father," Kirk assured him.

"I'll make sure you do," the king said. "But the damage has been done by this ad. It's really quite clever of the Gremlin."

"But most kids don't read the newspaper, do they, Father?" Kirk asked.

"That's true, Kirk," the king said. "But I'm worried that this isn't the only place this ad is running. Screen," he said, holding up the ad in the dining room, "show me any other places this ad appears."

Screen scanned the ad and returned a long list, including websites, stores, and public transportation sites. The king was even more agitated and began pacing.

"Can you ask these places to stop sharing the ad?" Kirk asked.

"I can and I will because of the harm it does to children. But many children have already seen it," the king said. He stopped his pacing and smiled. "Wait! I think there's something you can do to reverse the effects of this ad. You and the rest of the guardians can create an ad to promote reading."

"Great!" Ellen exclaimed. "But wait. What kind of ad? Should it just say 'Read books'?"

"That wouldn't be a very effective ad. I just realized I havent taught you three how to write ad copy," the king said. The king asked that *The Guidebook to Grammar Galaxy* be brought to him. He read the article on ad copy to the children.

Ad Copy

Ad copy is words written in an advertisement to create a desired action, often a sale.

The first step in creating ad copy that works is to consider your audience. Who are they and what do they want? What is their biggest problem? The ad should grab their attention based on that problem. Get your audience's attention by:

- identifying with their problem / reading their minds (*Your parents always complain that you don't read enough.*)

- giving an example person your audience can relate to (*Olivia was always late doing her homework until...*)

- asking a question (*Are you tired of the same old video games?*)

- **Citing a startling statistic** (*Reading just 4-5 books a summer can keep your reading skills strong.*)

Second, have one clear goal for your ad. Do you want your audience to change their minds, visit a website, or make a purchase? Your copy should reflect that goal.

Enroll in the free course that will show you how to create wealth. (goal: sign up for the course)

Third, reveal the greater purpose or benefit of taking action. Why should your audience care?

You'll have the knowledge and income you need, no matter what the future brings. (purpose: security)

Fourth, edit your ad to remove any unnecessary words. Can you make the same statement with fewer words?

Finally, test your ad copy. Does it get the results you want? If not, make changes and test it again.

"Is our audience for the ad kids our age?" Kirk asked.

"Indeed it is," the king answered.

"What do they need?" Luke asked.

"You can determine that by thinking about what you need or want," the king said.

"You know me. I want breakfast," Luke said. The rest of the family laughed.

"Think bigger, Luke. What do kids want?" the king asked.

"To have fun?" Luke suggested tentatively.

"Yes!" the king exclaimed.

"So we have to convince them that reading is fun," Kirk concluded.

"Or that they can have more fun if they read more," Ellen added.

"Now you're thinking," the king said. "I would like you three to create an ad that will get our young people reading this summer. In addition, I want you to send out a mission on writing ad copy. The guardians need to know who is behind the ad encouraging kids not read. We need lots of ads that will have the opposite effect."

The three English children had breakfast and got to work on an Ad Copy mission.

What does *pronto* mean?

Why was the king upset by the ad in the paper?

What is the first step in writing ad copy?

Chapter 36

"You surprised us!" the queen said as the king arrived at the breakfast table.

"Why, because I'm late for breakfast?" he asked, chuckling at his own joke.

"No, silly, because of the galactic holiday you declared. The kids are excited that there is no school. My friends are excited about the activities that are planned," the queen explained.

"And I'm excited about the food trucks! I love that stuff even though Cook says it's bad for me," Luke declared.

"Whoa, whoa, whoa. Wait a minute. What galactic holiday did I declare?" the king asked.

"Lipogram Day, of course. The children and I had no idea what it was. So I had the guidebook brought to us. Luke, read what a lipogram is for us again, would you?" the queen requested.

★ ★ ★ ★ ★ ★ ★ ★ ★ ★

obliged – *assisted*

★ ★ ★ ★ ★ ★ ★ ★ ★ ★

Luke **obliged** and read the entry.

Lipogram
A lipogram is a written work that excludes a letter or letters of the alphabet, typically the most common letters (*e, a, r, i, o, t, n, s, l*).   When early lipogram writers disliked a particular letter, they wrote without it. The best-known lipogram is Ernest Vincent Wright's novel *Gadsby*, which was written without the most common English letter: *e*.   Writing lipograms improves spelling and vocabulary. A good exercise is rewriting a version of a written work without the letter or letters you plan to remove.

"It's brilliant!" the queen gushed.

"Yes! Every hour, a new letter will be removed from our writing," Ellen added.

"I hope we can think of enough words without those missing letters," Luke said, worrying aloud.

"We can do it, Luke," Kirk reassured him. "It will stretch our vocabulary. And it will be fun," he said, smiling at his father.

"I'm pleased that you are enthusiastic about Lipogram Day. Writing lipograms is certainly a great way to improve spelling and vocabulary. There's just one problem," the king said, frowning. "I didn't declare it a galactic holiday."

His family gasped. "Then who did?" the queen said.

"One guess," the king said with **disparagement**.

"The Gremlin," his family said, groaning.

"Yes, the Gremlin. You said something about a schedule. May I see it?" the king asked.

★ ★ ★ ★ ★ ★ ★ ★ ★

disparagement – *scorn*

crestfallen – *disappointed*

★ ★ ★ ★ ★ ★ ★ ★ ★

The queen produced a flyer with the day's activities listed, which the king read. "They're going to remove *l* first. I'm worried that Lipogram Day isn't all fun and games. I think the Gremlin plans to send all these letters to planet Recycling. We wouldn't be able to use them even after Lipogram Day is over," the king said.

"Do you want us to go to planet Spelling to protect the letters?" Kirk volunteered.

"I appreciate your offer, Kirk. But I'm going to have Grammar Patrol handle it. I'll manage operations from here," the king said. Kirk nodded.

"Are you going to cancel Lipogram Day?" the queen asked, looking **crestfallen**.

The king thought for a moment and smiled. "I'm not."

Luke cheered. "Waffle cakes, here I come!"The family laughed.

"Why are you letting the holiday go on?" the queen asked her husband.

"The Gremlin meant this holiday to destroy our writing. And if he managed to remove our most popular letters, he would succeed. But lipograms are fun to write. And they do improve spelling and vocabulary skills. I want you to attend the celebration and have fun," the king said.

210

"Thank you, Father," Ellen said, hugging him.

"You're welcome," the king said warmly, hugging her back. "But I also have a mission for the three of you. I want you to have the guardians rewriting materials that will be a part of the celebration. If they don't, there will be confusion and chaos."

The three English children agreed and worked on a Lipogram mission. They sent it to the guardians before leaving for the holiday celebration.

What does *crestfallen* mean?

What was the king afraid the Gremlin would do on planet Spelling?

What is a lipogram?

About the Author

Dr. Melanie Wilson was a clinical psychologist working in a Christian practice, a college instructor, freelance writer, and public speaker before she felt called to stay home and educate her children. She is a mother of six and has homeschooled for 19 years. She says it's her most fulfilling vocation.

Melanie has always been passionate about language arts and used bits and pieces of different curriculum and approaches to teach her children and friends' children. In 2014, she believed she had another calling to write the curriculum she had always wanted as a homeschooling mom — one that didn't take a lot of time, made concepts simple and memorable, and was enough fun to keep her kids motivated.

Books have been a family business since the beginning. Melanie's husband Mark has been selling library books for 30 years. Melanie and the older kids frequently pitch in to help at the annual librarians' conference. *Grammar Galaxy* is another family business that she hopes will be a great learning opportunity for their children.

When Melanie isn't busy homeschooling, visiting her oldest sons in college, or writing, she loves to play tennis with family and friends.

Melanie is also the author of *Grammar Galaxy Nebula & Protostar, The Organized Homeschool Life* book and planner, and *So You're Not Wonder Woman*. She is the host of *The Homeschool Sanity Show* podcast and author of the blog, Psychowith6.com.

About the Illustrator

Rebecca Mueller has had an interest in drawing from an early age. Rebecca quickly developed a unique style and illustrated her first books, a short series of bedtime stories with her mother, at age 9. She has since illustrated for other authors and does graphic design work for several organizations. Rebecca is currently studying at the Pierre Laclede Honors College at the University of Missouri - St. Louis and is working towards a BA in English with a minor in Studio Art - Graphic Design.

Made in the USA
Monee, IL
13 June 2021